"If you're ready to change your narrative, Jon Acuff is here to help. A simple, powerful, and generous book, one that you'll remember every day for the rest of your life."

Seth Godin, author of *The Practice*

"Can science throw a party? Because that's what this book feels like. A smart, actionable, research-based party that makes you laugh hard and feel sad when it's over. I'll never think about thinking the same way."

Kendra Adachi, *New York Times* bestselling author
of *The Lazy Genius Way*

"Are you an overthinker? If you had to think about it, you should get Jon's new book."

Jim Gaffigan, comedian and author of *Food: A Love Story*

"Our thought life may be the most important and least considered part of our humanness and health. What Jon has done in this book is return us to the path of right thinking, which leads to healthier living and a more successful life. Jon Acuff is the guide we need right now for where we want to go and who we want to be, professionally and personally."

Annie F. Downs, bestselling author and host
of the *That Sounds Fun* podcast

"Jon Acuff has identified a hidden obstacle to success and produced a plan for knocking it down. So don't overthink the decision. Just pick up this practical, funny book and prepare to take notes."

Daniel H. Pink, *New York Times* bestselling author
of *When, Drive*, and *To Sell Is Human*

"I can't count the number of times I've told leaders, 'You're over-thinking that decision.' It's the natural enemy of focus, and I'm so glad Jon Acuff has jumped into the fray with a fresh perspective on this critical topic."

Michael Hyatt, *New York Times* bestselling author
of *The Vision Driven Leader*

"The cover's bright! The content's bright! The hope is bright! If you've ever wondered if it's possible to change the way you think and in doing so radically change your life, read *Soundtracks*. It's a book I hope everyone I know reads."

Bob Goff, Chief Balloon Inflator and *New York Times* bestselling
author of *Love Does*

"Good grief, Jon Acuff. Good grief! It's weird that you wrote this book exactly for me, but I have a feeling I'm not the only person who is going to think that. I knew I'd laugh. I knew I'd learn. What I didn't expect was to change the way I think about how I think. I'm going to be talking about this book for a long time."

Jen Hatmaker, *New York Times* bestselling author
of *Fierce, Free, and Full of Fire*

"There are few people as funny, witty, and thought-provoking as Jon Acuff. You learn deeply while simultaneously laughing and being engaged on all levels with his wisdom and story. *Soundtracks* is a powerful and necessary read."

Jefferson Bethke, *New York Times* bestselling author
of *Take Back Your Family*

"Your thoughts have power. I've spent decades on the water living by that principle. It's great to see Jon Acuff dive into the deep end about how important what we think really is with his new book *Soundtracks*."

Laird Hamilton, big wave surfer, innovator,
and cofounder of Laird SuperFood

"Overthinking is one of the natural enemies of essentialism. It's so encouraging to see Jon join the fight for work that matters with his new book *Soundtracks*."

Greg McKeown, host of the popular *What's Essential* podcast
and author of the *New York Times* bestseller
Essentialism: This Disciplined Pursuit of Less

"Jon takes our complicated thoughts and untangles them into a highway toward the best version of ourselves. *Soundtracks* will accelerate your mind and soul toward the confidence you have been looking for your whole life."

Carlos Whittaker, author of *Enter Wild, Kill the Spider,*
and *Moment Maker*

"We all struggle with those self-discouraging messages we listen to in our heads. They make us overthink everything, and they get in the way of great relationships and visionary goals. Jon Acuff's book provides a clear skill map to redirect our minds to create truly transformational messages that can and will change everything. Jon's content is a rare combination of researched practical help along with a warm and funny style. You will never regret reading *Soundtracks*."

John Townsend, PhD, *New York Times* bestselling author
of the *Boundaries* series; founder of the Townsend
Institute for Leadership and Counseling
and the Townsend Leadership Program

"We need this book right now. Jon Acuff will change the way you think, act, and succeed!"

Vanessa Van Edwards, bestselling author of *Captivate: The Science of Succeeding with People*

"Jon Acuff's latest release awed me immediately. The combination of compelling stories and sound research make *Soundtracks* what I believe to be Acuff's best book to date—and that's saying a lot! He not only identifies evidence of the flawed thinking many of us have come to believe is simply inherent, he offers real-world solutions to changing our thought processes into productive fuel. This is the book Jon Acuff was born to write."

Andy Andrews, *New York Times* bestselling author
of *The Traveler's Gift*, *The Noticer*, and *Just Jones*

"Is it possible to stop overthinking, increase your confidence, and actually accomplish the work you dream of doing? Jon Acuff proves it can be done. *Soundtracks* is like the ideal mix tape with just the right amount of actionable advice, keen insight, and hilarious anecdotes to make you want to rewind and play it again . . . this time at full volume."

Tanya Dalton, bestselling author of *The Joy of Missing Out*

"Jon Acuff marched into the jungle of overthinking with a machete of simplicity and carved a beautifully written path we can all follow. If you've got a goal to crush and want your thoughts to work for you, not against you, read *Soundtracks* as fast as you can."

Lindsay Teague Moreno, bestselling author of *Boss Up*

"I picked up *Soundtracks* at one in the morning when I was having my nightly mental chatter that I couldn't turn off. Within the first few pages, Jon delivered a life-changing discovery: I am bigger than my brain. If you're looking to embrace the power of thought to work *for* you and not *against* you, *Soundtracks* is the book you need."

Jess Ekstrom, author of *Chasing the Bright Side*

"The best thing about this book is that Jon Acuff makes it so much fun to read, it doesn't feel like work. But when you're done reading, you're a different, wiser, more activated person. It's like if you could just think about going to the gym and end up with a beach body."

Brian Koppelman, co-creator and writer of *Billions* and *Rounders*

"Smart people aren't supposed to be this funny. Funny people aren't supposed to be this smart. Jon Acuff somehow got both skills, and I'm so glad he did. You will be too once you read *Soundtracks*."

Sam Collier, bestselling author of *A Greater Story*

"Another home run from Jon Acuff. How you allocate your finite attention is critical to success and life satisfaction. Wasting mental cycles on overthinking is akin to wasting your life. *Soundtracks* shares simple and effective strategies for quieting the noise and zeroing in on what matters most."

Todd Henry, author of *The Motivation Code*

"In a world filled with adversity, negativity, and distractions, Jon Acuff has written a revolutionary book that will help you have more clarity, focus, and power to take on your challenges and win the battle of your mind. He brilliantly shares how you can turn overthinking from a super problem into a superpower! This book is a must-read!"

Jon Gordon, bestselling author of *The Energy Bus* and *The Garden*

"Yuck. Jon Acuff. How does he do it? He's as funny as he is helpful. He makes you laugh but then makes you completely rethink your life. As if that weren't envy-inducing enough, he's actually written one of his best books yet. *Soundtracks* is rich with insight and reads like a note from a trusted friend—who also happens to be disgustingly talented."

Brad Montague, guy behind *Kid President* and author of *Becoming Better Grownups*

"All my life I've dealt with negative self-talk and discouraging thoughts, but I never understood why. After reading *Soundtracks*, not only do I understand myself better, I also know how to rewire the negativity. When Jon asked me to write an endorsement for this book, I didn't need to overthink it."

Chris Guillebeau, author of *The Money Tree* and *The $100 Startup*

soundtracks

soundtracks

The Surprising Solution to **Overthinking**

JON ACUFF

BakerBooks
a division of Baker Publishing Group
Grand Rapids, Michigan

Published by Baker Books
a division of Baker Publishing Group
PO Box 6287, Grand Rapids, MI 49516-6287
www.bakerbooks.com

Printed in the United States of America

Library of Congress Cataloging-in-Publication Data
Names: Acuff, Jonathan, author.
Title: Soundtracks : the surprising solution to overthinking / Jon Acuff.
Description: Grand Rapids, Michigan : Baker Books, a division of Baker Publishing Group, 2021.
Identifiers: LCCN 2020035482 | ISBN 9781540900807 (cloth) | ISBN 9781540901408 (paperback)
Subjects: LCSH: Thought and thinking. | Fear. | Success.
Classification: LCC BF441 .A264 2021 | DDC 153.4/2—dc23
LC record available at https://lccn.loc.gov/2020035482

Some names and identifying details have been changed to protect the privacy of individuals.

Published in association with Yates & Yates, www.yates2.com.

Interior design by William Overbeeke.

21 22 23 24 25 26 27   7 6 5 4 3 2 1

"Jon, I think you might be
overthinking this."
—Jenny Acuff

Contents

Introduction

I waited thirteen years to share this secret.

I apologize for taking so long, but it seemed too good to be true.

I kept thinking the other shoe was going to drop. The secret seemed so simple and so obvious that at first I thought I was wrong.

Maybe it was a fluke. Maybe it worked for me because my situation was unique. Maybe everything that happened was an accident, and if I tried to teach someone else how to do it, it wouldn't help. Maybe if I shared it, people would think I was weird. The neon-green shoes are certainly unusual. The coin is a bit of a surprise. The Post-it notes are a thing. Better to keep it to myself.

So I did.

This secret moved me to Nashville.

It helped me hit the *New York Times* bestseller list.

It sent me to Portugal and Greece and even many parts of Canada that I can't tell you about because it would melt your face right off.

For thirteen years I kept this secret in my back pocket, using it to transform my career, my relationships, my health, and every other part of my life.

Eventually though, I got curious. Was I the only one this secret could help? I launched a survey with my researcher, Mike Peasley, PhD, and asked ten thousand people if they struggle with the thing I figured out. More than 99.5 percent of them said yes.

Okay, okay, so I'm not the only one.

I still wasn't ready to share the whole secret, so I cut off a sliver and tested that with thousands of people from around the world. Mike Peasley, PhD, analyzed the results, and we were both shocked at what happened. I mean genuinely surprised, not Buzzfeed "You'll be shocked at what this celebrity's feet look like" surprised.

I'm also going to use Mike Peasley, PhD's full name, including his doctorate, every time I mention him because at times in this book you'll be tempted to think, "This writing is so delightful, there's no way it can also be scientific." But it is. Ask Mike Peasley, PhD. He was there.

After thirteen years I'm finally ready. If you'll lean in close, I'll tell you what the secret is:

I discovered how to turn overthinking from a super problem into a superpower.

1. I Think I Can Do This

Overthinking is when what you think gets in the way of what you want.

It's one of the most expensive things in the world because it wastes time, creativity, and productivity. It's an epidemic of inaction, a tsunami of stuckness, and thirteen years ago it was dominating me.

I was the king of someday, high on thought, low on motion about a litany of things I'd do eventually.

"Quit overthinking so much," coworkers would beg.

"It's all in your head," my wife would implore.

"Get out of your own way," schoolchildren would yell as I stumbled through the streets like a heavy-brained monster.

Did I want to have 1,345 thoughts about whether there would be adequate parking at the new restaurant we were going to? Did I want to donate an afternoon of brain space to reviewing something dumb I said to a friend three months ago in the grocery store? Did I want to put off asking for a raise for one more month, overthinking the myriad ways it could go wrong?

Of course not, but what could I do? Thoughts are something you have, not something you hone. We can't control them, right? That's why whenever we talk about thinking, we describe it as something outside of us that operates on its own agenda:

"I got lost in my thoughts."

"My thoughts got away from me."

"She got carried away by her thoughts."

Even if we are very deliberate in other areas of our lives, we tend to treat our thought life as something we have no control over. For example, a simple trick to ensure you go to the gym in the morning is to lay out your workout clothes the night before. Picking them ahead of time helps you achieve the result you want.

> **Overthinking is when what you think gets in the way of what you want.**

Have you ever heard someone say that about thoughts? "Make sure you pick the five thoughts you want to have playing in the background of your head in that meeting tomorrow." Has a coworker ever said, "I heard some gossip about our new manager, but I don't want that to color our relationship, so I'm going to leave my three judgmental thoughts at home so I can get to know her without any bias"?

No one has ever said anything like that to me. If we don't control our thoughts, then I guess our thoughts control us. No wonder I spent decades overthinking every little decision,

16

never fully pulling the trigger on the things I really wanted to accomplish.

One afternoon, out of the clear blue, I got an email from a marketing coordinator in Oklahoma. He'd been reading my blog and asked me a question I never saw coming:

"Can you speak at our conference?"

The answer should have been, "No." I'd never been paid to speak before. I'd never written a speech with main ideas and transitions. I'd never worked with an event planner. I'd never been to Oklahoma, though I assumed it was very dusty.

At the time, I had a ten-year history of making small, incremental changes in my career as a corporate copywriter who never spoke publicly.

If you looked for evidence that I was a public speaker, there was none.

The only thing I had was a new thought: *I think I can do this.*

I chose one small thought, which led to one small yes, which led to a completely different life.

Long before a single speech, long before I wrote a book that the NFL Players Association teaches players, long before I opened for Dolly Parton at the Ryman, I changed the way I thought about what I was capable of, and that changed everything.

That day I took the first step toward learning something amazing: you can control your thoughts.

You can turn overthinking into action. You can use all that reclaimed time, creativity, and productivity to create the life you want.

And it starts with recognizing your thoughts for what they really are—a personal soundtrack for your life.

The Soundtracks That Are Secretly Shaping Your Life

If I hear "Sweet Child O' Mine" by Guns N' Roses, I can smell the newsprint from the pages of *Thrasher* magazine. I can see myself sitting on the floor at 2 Edgewood Drive in Hudson, Massachusetts, cutting out photos of skateboarders for my bulletin board. That's when you really knew you were Sk8 or Die, when you maintained a suburban scrapbook of California skaters.

If I hear "It Takes Two" by Rob Base and DJ EZ Rock, I am instantly transported to Dave Bruce's basement. We are memorizing the lyrics as fast as we can, shouting them back and forth to each other and wishing we were rich enough to own Z. Cavaricci pants. I'm not internationally known, but I'm known to rock the microphone.

If I hear "Mr. Jones" by Counting Crows, I can see myself in the Framingham Mall parking lot trying to get my date to listen to the lyrics. I'm in my mom's blue minivan with faux wood paneling, and it's bothering me that Heather isn't as moved by Adam Duritz as I am. It wasn't easy to rewind tapes. It was a very imprecise art, and the longer she talked over the song, the harder it was for me to find the part I wanted her to really connect with.

Those songs are from bands that will probably never share a stage. I can't see Counting Crows doing a collab with Guns N' Roses. But what they all have in common is that they each hit me at the sweet spot when soundtracks are formed.

The *New York Times* did a study to figure out when a song has the greatest shot at getting added to your permanent soundtrack, that list of songs that will always impact you. The title of the article that followed was "The Songs That Bind," and it's a fitting description of what a soundtrack does. Using data from Spotify, economist Seth Stephens-Davidowitz found that "the most important period for men in forming their adult tastes were the ages 13 to 16." For women, it skews a little earlier, with the ages 11 to 14 being most important.[1]

Just reading my list of three examples probably called to mind a specific song and memory for you.

The playlist you unknowingly curate during your life makes for an interesting dinner party conversation, but music is only one small part of a much bigger story. Your thoughts are the internal soundtracks you listen to even more than your favorite song.

Over the years, you've built a soundtrack about your career. You have a soundtrack for all your relationships. You have a soundtrack you believe about your hopes, dreams, goals, and every other aspect of your life.

If you listen to any thought long enough, it becomes a part of your personal playlist.

Soundtracks made of music have the ability to completely transform a moment. Restaurants know this. Movies know this. Gyms know this.

No offense to Slash, but soundtracks made of thoughts are even more powerful. They're much bigger than just background music. As retired Navy SEAL David Goggins says, "The most important conversations you'll ever have are the ones you'll have with yourself. You wake up with them, you walk around with them, you go to bed with them and

If you **listen**
to any thought
long enough,
it becomes a part
of your **personal**
playlist.

eventually you learn to act on them. Whether they be good or bad."[2]

If the soundtracks you listen to are positive, your thoughts can be your best friend, propelling you on new adventures with creativity and hope. If your day is spent overthinking broken soundtracks, your thoughts can be your worst foe, holding you back from ever taking action on all the things you want in life.

Decades before Bluetooth and Sirius XM, my college roommate Stu had a car with a broken radio that would only play one station—Disney Radio. That's not a problem if you're a parent, because any Peppa Pig in a storm will do, but it's a little creepy if you're cruising around campus blasting Hannah Montana.

My roommate didn't have any control over that soundtrack, and most of the time that's how we think about our thoughts too. We don't think we can change them, so we tend to leave our soundtracks up to chance.

Unfortunately, when you don't create, curate, and choose what soundtracks you'll listen to, the music doesn't stop. You just hear a bunch of songs you don't like.

Your Brain Can Be a Real Jerk

Let's start with something we all agree on: you and I have brains. They are capable of some amazing things, like logic, reason, and Mariah Carey's "All I Want for Christmas Is You." That song has made her an estimated $60 million in royalties.[3] Don't you dare tell me it's not amazing.

One of the things our brains are capable of is overthinking. Think of it as the ability to have persistent, repetitive thoughts.

Overthinking is essentially when your brain spins on a thought or an idea for longer than you anticipated. Unfortunately, overthinking tends to lean toward the negative. Left to its own devices, it will naturally gravitate toward things you don't want to dwell on. I'll give you a few examples.

Have you ever had to work hard to remind yourself of something dumb you said a long time ago? Did you need a to-do list to overthink an embarrassing situation from the eighth grade, even though you're now in your thirties? Did you need a note on your calendar to make sure you'd spend the whole weekend thinking about why your boss called a meeting with you on Monday morning?

"I've got a wave of dread scheduled for this Saturday at 2 p.m.!" Is that what you did, or did those thoughts just show up unexpectedly, not at all connected to anything else you were doing at the time?

Those are called *broken soundtracks*, negative stories you tell yourself about yourself and your world. They play automatically without any invitation or effort from you. Fear does not take work. Doubt does not take work. Insecurity does not take work.

I know all about broken soundtracks like that because they cost me seven years of opportunity.

I started my first blog in 2001. I was sharing ridiculous, personal content online three years before Facebook existed, four years before YouTube, five years before Twitter, and sixteen years before TikTok. I wasn't a tech pioneer, because I didn't own enough hoodies, but I was way ahead of the curve. Record labels were reaching out, readers were finding the content organically, and the faintest hints of momentum were sprouting. Things were moving along, but then I started overthinking everything.

"What if someone finds out I don't really know what I'm doing?"

"Where is this even going?"

"What's the point if I don't have a perfect plan to grow it?"

Those three soundtracks and a thousand more knocked me off the internet for seven straight years. I didn't start another blog until 2008. Who knows how much further I'd be if I'd spent those seven years growing my audience and content?

The most frustrating thing is that all those broken soundtracks showed up in my life completely uninvited.

Paul Rozin, a psychology professor at the University of Chicago, studied this phenomenon when he realized that the English language doesn't even have a word that means the opposite of trauma. Roy F. Baumeister, Rozin's collaborator, explained why in his book *The Power of Bad: How the Negativity Effect Rules Us and How We Can Rule It*: "There is no opposite of trauma, because no single good event has such a lasting impact. You can consciously recall happy moments from your past, but the ones that suddenly pop into your head uninvited—the involuntary memories, as psychologists call them—tend to be unhappy."[4]

Your brain builds on overthinking's habit of negativity by doing three additional things:

1. Lying about your memories
2. Confusing fake trauma with real trauma
3. Believing what it already believes

We often think our memory is like a GoPro, just capturing things as they happen in real time for later review. Simple things, complex things, happy things, painful things—it's all just one long film of our life that we can access later. If only that were the case.

In his podcast *Revisionist History*, Malcolm Gladwell brings his world-renowned brand of insight to the topic of memory. In one episode, he does the unexpected and attempts to exonerate news reporter Brian Williams.

Williams was riding high as the host of *NBC Nightly News* when his whole career came tumbling down with a preposterous lie. On March 23, 2013, he told David Letterman that he had been on a Chinook helicopter that was fired on by enemy troops in Iraq ten years earlier. That seems like the kind of thing one would remember. For instance, I know right now, I haven't been on a helicopter that was attacked by a rocket-propelled grenade. You probably do too. But Williams thought he was. How could he possibly get something so big, so wrong?

Flashbulb Memories Make Us Blind to the Truth

In his podcast episode, Gladwell talked to memory experts who expressed empathy for Williams. They pointed to the considerable research around so-called flashbulb memories, dramatic experiences that create a vivid recollection in our heads.

Some flashbulb memories are shared by an entire country. William Hirst and a team of researchers did a ten-year study into the memories people have of 9/11. If I asked you right now where you were when the towers fell, you'd probably be able to remember. I was unemployed at home in Arlington, Massachusetts, listening to the radio.

The problem is that as Hirst studied the memories of the participants over the years, he discovered something surprising: they changed. As time passed, the details of what they remembered morphed. And not just a little bit. Hirst found on average "a 60% decline in memory consistency. Meaning 60% of the answers changed over time."[5]

The crazy thing is that even as the accuracy of our memories declines, our confidence in them doesn't. In 1986, on the day after the space shuttle *Challenger* explosion, Nicole Harsch and Ulric Neisser asked psychology students how they heard the tragic news. The students wrote down their answers. Nearly three years later, the researchers asked those same students that same question. More than 40 percent of the students answered the question differently the second time because their memories had changed.

The researchers pointed out to participants that the two memories they wrote down were different. They showed them the initial memories they themselves had written down. Confused participants admitted the handwriting was theirs but still wouldn't admit their memories were inaccurate. They said, "I agree it's my handwriting. I agree I must have written that. I don't know why I lied, because I clearly remember I was in the dorm even though this piece of paper says I was in the cafeteria."[6]

One of the things that causes flashbulb memories is "the degree to which the memory of the event is rehearsed, i.e., how often are people likely to recall the event?"[7]

That's overthinking's favorite jam.

Can you imagine something you rehearse more than the negative soundtracks in your head? That's what overthinking does. It finds a negative soundtrack and then plays it over and over again. I've listened to "Sweet Child O' Mine" a thousand times. I've listened to "That friend didn't respond to your text message because they're mad" a hundred thousand times.

The memory doesn't have to be as tragic as 9/11 or the *Challenger* explosion. Have you ever been fired? Have you ever been dumped? Did a coworker ever yell at you in a meeting? Did you ever miss a flight because you overslept? Those might not seem like significant events compared to national tragedies, but that's when your brain leans into the second reason it's kind of a jerk: you have a hard time distinguishing real trauma from fake trauma.

Researchers at the University of Michigan Medical School found that when we experience a social rejection, our brain releases the same kind of opioids it releases during a physical trauma. Even when the participants knew ahead of time that the social rejection was fake and part of a study, the result was the same. Our brain hits the panic button and dumps opioids into our body to help us survive the perceived emotional pain.[8]

When faced with fake rejection, your body releases real chemicals.

As a parent, it's so tempting to tell your kids it's no big deal when they share something they're worried about. In the grand scheme of things, losing your favorite seat at the lunch table when you're a high school sophomore is insignificant. But a lot more is going on than just a cafeteria misunderstanding. That sixteen-year-old daughter is awash in real opioids indicating real danger. It's very much a big deal.

So our memory lies, and our brain has a hard time telling the difference between real trauma and fake trauma. Those two challenges are daunting enough. Now comes the third member of the overthinking trifecta: confirmation bias.

Our brain likes to believe the things it already believes.

We're magnets for information and experiences that confirm the things we already think about ourselves and the world. If one of your soundtracks is that you're the most disorganized mom ever, then being three minutes late to the after-school pickup line will confirm that. Even if that morning you got both kids to school on time, worked a full-time job, planned dinner, and scheduled weekend carpooling for a soccer tournament, your brain will still convince you to ignore any new evidence that doesn't agree with your broken soundtrack.

The Power Is Yours

Now that you know your brain can be a real jerk, do you want to leave your thoughts to chance? Where would successful people be if they hadn't made a decision to choose new soundtracks to listen to? Think of all the opportunities and adventures you'll miss out on if broken soundtracks are in charge of your actions.

Broken soundtracks are one of the most persuasive forms of fear because every time you listen to one it gets easier to believe it the next time. Have you ever judged an idea as too dumb to even write down? That's a broken soundtrack. Have you ever told yourself the same story I do about why someone didn't text back? That's a broken soundtrack. Has it ever felt like you have a pocket jury with you, cross-examining each new opportunity until you dare not chase it? That's a broken soundtrack.

The good news is that you're bigger than your brain. It's just one part of you, and it's under your control in the same way an arm or leg is. We know this because you and I have the great fortune of living in the age of neuroplasticity. Your parents' generation didn't know they could change the shape and function of their brains. Their parents' generation thought cigarettes were good for cyclists in the Tour de France because the nicotine opened the capillaries in their lungs. Maybe my kids' generation will be the ones who figure out how to make vegan queso not taste like organic sand. Every generation learns something new.

Neuroplasticity, which is the power to physically change our brains by changing our thoughts, means that the solution to overthinking isn't to stop thinking. Why would we ever get rid of such a powerful, efficient tool? Wouldn't it make more sense to just run our brains with different soundtracks instead of the broken ones? A plane can drop a bomb or food. A syringe can deliver poison or medicine. A stallion can start a stampede or win a race. The same is true of our thoughts.

If you can worry, you can wonder. If you can doubt, you can dominate. If you can spin, you can soar.

The same brain that told you for years that you couldn't write a book can be taught to tell you just the opposite. "You can write a book! You must write a book! It's time to do it!"

I should know. I published zero books the first thirty-three years of my life. I published seven over the next eleven years. How? I started listening to a new soundtrack.

I didn't just give myself a boost of encouragement in 2008 when I chose to believe I could become a professional public speaker. I started changing my soundtracks in ways that changed the shape of my brain. Not just one day but

If you can worry, you can wonder. If you can doubt, you can dominate. If you can spin, you can soar.

every day, which was all the easier because of neurogenesis. With neurogenesis, "every morning when you wake up, new baby nerve cells have been born while you were sleeping that are there at your disposal to be used in tearing down toxic thoughts and rebuilding healthy thoughts."[9]

Your brain is waiting for you each day. It's waiting to be told what to think. It's waiting to see what kind of soundtracks you'll choose.

It's waiting to see if you really want to build a different life.

Changing Your Thoughts When Your Circumstances Change

It's one thing to choose a positive soundtrack and then use it to create something good. But what about the reverse? Can soundtracks help us escape from bad situations? What role do they play when life doesn't go the way you want? How can you use your thoughts to rebuild something that's fallen apart?

Colleen Barry faced these questions when she lost her job in Boston as a result of the dot-com bust in 2001. She had to take three jobs to cobble together what her previous salary as a documentary film researcher and distributor used to cover.

One of her jobs was to answer the phones as the receptionist in a small office for Gibson Sotheby's International Realty. "It was not the direction I wanted to go," she told me. "I was trying to move into a creative field, not make minimum wage answering phones." Overthinking could have gotten very loud in that moment and played any number of soundtracks.

Entitlement: "I shouldn't have to answer phones; this work is beneath me."

Regret: "My last job was so much better than these other three I have to work just to get by."

Fear: "What if the economy collapses again and I lose these jobs as well?"

Blame: "It's not my fault I lost my job. Life is so unfair."

Resignation: "This is how things will be forever."

Instead of listening to any of those broken soundtracks, Colleen decided to look at the situation with fresh eyes. "I discovered something: I was doing this job as much for me as I was doing it for them." She said, "If I wanted to grow, I had to make the path, because there was no clear path from just answering the phones. The company wasn't going to give me a path. If I wanted to find the path and enjoy the day, I had to change things."

Colleen's dreams had been knocked off course, but she decided to control the things she could control.

"Instead of being disappointed that my career took a step backward, I decided to make it my job to offer the best customer service I could."

She made a choice. Instead of listening to a soundtrack that said, "I have a menial job," she came up with her own soundtrack: "My job is to offer the best customer service." A thousand other people in that situation would let the circumstances dictate their soundtracks, as evidenced by every sandwich some grumpy person has served me in airport food courts, but Colleen did just the opposite.

Once you've picked the right soundtrack, it gets easier to pick the right actions.

That's always how it goes. Your thoughts empower your actions, which in turn generate your results. "I leveraged a connection to get us a coffee machine and pods. I offered every visitor to the office an espresso or cappuccino," Colleen said. The tired, stressed-out customers noticed a difference. After a long day of seeing expensive rental properties in a city where finding a place to live is a competitive sport, weary clients would return to the real estate office and be welcomed into Colleen's sanctuary.

> **Your thoughts empower your actions, which in turn generate your results.**

That's a nice story, isn't it? Colleen, answering phones politely and offering espressos to customers who weren't expecting such great customer service? The story doesn't end there though.

Colleen became the CEO.

Please try not to step on the mic I just dropped.

It's true. Colleen changed her soundtrack, which changed her actions, which changed her life, and today she's the firm's CEO.

Did it happen overnight? Of course not. It took fifteen years. I don't care how amazing your coffee is, no one jumps from lobby barista to CEO in a week. It took me six years to become a full-time public speaker, though I think the New Anthem in chapter 8 will help you shave some time off your journey.

Colleen got an entry-level marketing position. Then she ended up running the marketing department. Next, she jumped to business coaching, all while writing fresh soundtracks that moved her forward. For example, she doesn't just see coworkers when she shows up on a Monday morning. "I imagine that everyone I work with is a business partner that I'm trying to help grow. I have 350 partners."

Was it always easy? Nope. She says that after the dot-com bust, everybody was pretty depressed. "We had all come from making lots of money in fancy offices that had ping-pong and pool tables. You had to make a decision: will I just try to collect unemployment, or will I do the work the way I really want to do it?"

Did Colleen ever get annoyed answering the phones? She did. "There were a couple of times when it was frustrating, and I would think, 'Really? This is what my life has come to? I was in Cannes a year ago, showing a film.'" She didn't keep listening to that broken soundtrack though.

"I have to be very cautious about taking a thing that I'm experiencing in the moment and then making it the permanent thing. Our brains do that. But it's not the new normal, you're just having a crappy day."

You're going to have a few of those moments. Everybody does.

Three months into believing I could be a professional public speaker, I attended an event and planned a meet-up for all the people who were reading my blog. I wasn't speaking at the event because no one but me knew I was a public speaker yet, but the staff allowed me to use an empty room at the arena.

I printed out a thousand stickers and brought a dump truck's worth of Skittles because I'd written a joke about them that I thought was funny. I waited in the room for readers to show up, expecting a massive crowd. In ninety minutes, do you know how many people came through those doors? Two. One was a friend named Mike Foster who happened to be at the event. The other was a father who walked in and said, "I don't read your blog, but my daughter does. Call her." He then handed me his phone, I had an awkward thirty-second conversation with his daughter, and then he left. I think he took a sticker.

If I listened to my broken soundtracks, that day was an abject failure. Only two people attended my event. If that same thing happened to me in my twenties, that embarrassment would have become one more reminder that overthinking played whenever I tried to do something brave. I would have quit that foolish dream like I quit my first blog, potentially sacrificing another seven years to being stuck.

But this time was different. I was controlling my soundtracks instead of letting them control me. Instead of giving up, I chose to play my new soundtrack at full blast: "YOU CAN BE A PUBLIC SPEAKER AND AUTHOR!"

Instead of feeling crushed that day, I recognized it for what it was: a chance to share an experience with other people—failure. I had my friend take a photo of me surrounded by a sea of empty chairs. That night I wrote about the experience, and it became one of my most popular blog posts ever.

Eleven years later, I stood onstage in front of eight thousand people and smiled about something no one else knew. I was in the very same arena I'd been in when my meet-up failed. I was about five hundred yards from the spot where I had to carry 999 stickers back to my car.

To be clear, I didn't have a perfect plan that carried me from the failed meet-up to the keynote on the main stage. All I had was the soundtrack that told me it was possible.

Tapping Into the Power of Overthinking in Three Steps

My entire world started to change when I decided to choose what soundtracks I listen to.

The best part is that the process is a lot simpler than you'd expect. When I first started transforming my overthinking, I figured it would take approximately ninety-two different steps, fourteen techniques, and at least a few dozen acronyms. I was wrong.

There are three actions to change your thoughts from a super problem into a superpower:

1. Retire your broken soundtracks.
2. Replace them with new ones.
3. Repeat them until they're as automatic as the old ones.

Retire. Replace. Repeat.

That's it.

I don't know what your dream is; it's probably different from mine. But I do know one thing: overthinking is getting in the way.

It's time to do something about that.

2. The Choice Is Yours

Don't ever leave your pregnant wife at the bottom of the Duomo in Florence, Italy, because you felt like the walls of the tower were closing in on you and the only way to alleviate that thought was to sprint up the 463 marble steps and burst through the door onto the rooftop deck like Tim Robbins at the end of the pipe escape scene in *The Shawshank Redemption*.

That's the longest sentence I've ever written and oddly specific advice, but I wish someone had told me that in 2003. That was five years before I started transforming my overthinking, and my runaway thoughts were still running the show, even on vacation.

My problem started a few weeks before we left for the trip, when I had a conversation with my dad. He told me, "Be careful about that Duomo. The tower up to the top is really narrow. Two people can barely pass each other on that massive spiral staircase. Once you're in the middle of it, you're a long way from either the exit or the entrance. There aren't even windows, just these tiny slits in the wall to the outside. The whole thing is dark and damp and made me feel claustrophobic."

Fantastic.

That was music to overthinking's ears. A soundtrack immediately took up residence in my head. For weeks, I listened to "You'll feel stuck in the Duomo" on repeat. By the time we got to Italy, I was, as they say in the south, "Fit to be tied."

I started looking at how narrow the whole structure was. "My dad was right," I thought, "this is like climbing inside a vertical cigarette from the fourteenth century. Am I even making any progress? Without windows I can't tell if I'm getting higher. I feel like an Italian hamster just going around and around the same spot. Do I have vertigo right now? If my phone had a signal, I could check my symptoms on WebMD. Wait, I don't have any signal? If I collapse, I can't contact anyone and will have to hope the rats I encounter aren't so obsessed with making ratatouille that they're too busy to carry an SOS note to my wife. Why did I fly all the way around the world to feel like this when I could have just crawled inside a rolled-up rug in IKEA for free? I'm trapped!"

As my soundtrack started to spin faster, so did my legs. I don't remember when I decided to sprint up the stairs, but there I was, dodging tourists and fighting my way to the top of the tower. I left my six-months-pregnant wife below me in the dust as I climbed higher into the heavens, desperate to find the door leading to fresh air and salvation.

"What was that all about?" Jenny asked me twenty minutes later when she finally made it to the top like a normal person. I tried to brush it off but was too sweaty to pretend I hadn't just set a Mediterranean land speed record for stair climbing. I didn't have an answer for her at the time because I hadn't studied overthinking yet. But knowing what I know now, I should have apologized and told her the crazy story I'm about to tell you.

The Science behind Replacing Your Soundtracks

"Sticks and stones may break my bones but words will never hurt me" is a fun phrase to say, but it's not even a little bit true. Words are so powerful that they can age you faster than that one guy who chose the wrong chalice in *Indiana Jones and the Last Crusade*.

Scientists studied that exact scenario at New York University.[1] I don't think the name of the study was "Will words age people faster than that one guy in the *Last Crusade*?," but that's what they found. The researchers started the study by giving two different groups of students the same assignment: make sentences out of a collection of seemingly random words.

Both groups proceeded to make as many sentences as they could, but there was something slightly different about the words the second group of students was given. Hidden in that group of words were ideas that were related to old age. Words such as "bald," "Florida," and "wrinkle" were sprinkled throughout their collection.

At the end of the word challenge, the scientists told the participants to walk down the hall to complete the second portion of the study in another classroom. As they made their way down, the real test began. Scientists secretly timed the students to see how long it took them to make the short trip. The students exposed to the set of old-age words walked slower.

Just reading the words about being elderly caused a physical change. This is a form of priming, which Nobel Prize winner Daniel Kahneman defines as "the influencing of an action by the idea."[2] Priming's formal name is the *ideomotor effect*, and it works both ways. Your thoughts and ideas influence your actions. Your actions influence your thoughts. That's why replacing broken soundtracks is so important.

A team in Germany demonstrated the ideomotor effect when they reversed the NYU study. This time researchers had one group of participants walk around the room slower than they normally would and the other group walk at their usual gait. When shown a word bank, the group who walked slower was quicker at finding words related to being old. The act of physically slowing down improved their ability to find words their brains thought of as slow. In essence, "If you were primed to think of old age, you would tend to act old, and acting old would reinforce the thought of old age."[3]

Why was it so easy for me to run up the stairs at the Duomo? Why did that action feel so automatic while at the same time catch me off guard? Because I was primed. For weeks, overthinking had been telling me, "You'll feel stuck in that tower." As soon as I put my foot on that first step, all those broken soundtracks rushed in.

I shouldn't have been surprised at that reaction. What you think influences what you do, which influences the results you get. I knew that. I think I've always known that, but I didn't know the power hidden in that principle until 2008.

If my soundtracks could encourage me to run up the steps at the Duomo, could they also encourage me to walk up the steps onstage at speaking events?

If my soundtracks could make me hyperfocus on a fear like getting stuck in the tower, could they also make me hyperfocus on a goal like writing a book?

If my soundtracks could make an entire cathedral disappear in worry, could they also make a mountain of obstacles disappear in hope?

Spoiler alert: the answer is yes, or else this is the worst book ever.

When you pick the soundtracks you listen to the most, there's no limit to what you can accomplish.

> **When you pick the soundtracks you listen to the most, there's no limit to what you can accomplish.**

Now you know why I didn't write about this for thirteen years. It seems way too simple and obvious. So why don't more people work on their overthinking?

Because everyone has too many thoughts and doesn't know where to start.

The Three Questions You Should Ask Your Soundtracks

In 1968, Pyotr Anokhin, a student of psychological pioneer Ivan Pavlov, "published research demonstrating that the minimum number of potential thought patterns the average brain can make in a lifetime is the number 1 followed by 10.5 million kilometers of typewritten zeros."[4]

I converted the kilometers to miles because I'm still bucking the metric system in a very aggressive way, and that equals the number 1 followed by 6.5 million miles of zeros. That's how big the number of your thought patterns is. No wonder most people get discouraged when they think about overthinking. If a friend said, "Can I talk to you about something? Actually, 6.5 million miles of somethings," that'd be an overwhelming conversation.

Who has time for that? I don't. You don't either. Wouldn't it be a lot easier if we just asked our loudest soundtracks three quick questions to determine which ones we should listen to?

Question 1: Is it true?

One of the greatest mistakes you can make in life is assuming all your thoughts are true. We tend to believe that if it's in our head, it must be accurate. If I think it, it must be real. Despite the wild things our thoughts have told us over the years, we trust them. When you start to ask a soundtrack this question, I promise you'll be shocked by how many lies you have cluttering up your head.

When I asked Cody Skog what he was overthinking, he said, "I overthink doing magic for paid events." An amateur magician, his goal was to start doing more paid events. The broken soundtrack he heard was, "You can't charge for your services because someone else might be better at magic."

The tricky thing—some degree of pun intended—is that there's a small bit of truth to that. If overthinking was purely a lie, it would be easy to beat. But it's true, there are going to be better magicians than Cody. That's true of any profession.

One of the
GREATEST
MISTAKES
you can make in life
is assuming all your
thoughts are **true.**

There are better writers than me. That's not false humility; that's a fact. But what was Cody's soundtrack really saying?

When we pull the thread, we see that the broken soundtrack "You can't charge for your services because someone else might be better at magic" is actually saying, "Until no one else in the world is better than you, you can't do magic for paid events." So now all Cody has to do is become the greatest magician in the entire world before he charges for his work. This is of course impossible, because to become the best in the world he'd need to do paid events to finance his march to the top. What a perfect overthinking loop that is.

Let's run his soundtrack through our first filter: Is it true?

Is it true that you have to be the best magician in the world before you charge people? Is there some sort of official magic tournament you have to win to be crowned greatest? Or is it like the movie *Highlander* and you have to travel from city to city, vanquishing each magician one by one and stealing their power until at last you stand on a mossy heath and proclaim, "I can now make money via magic!"

The answer is obvious. That soundtrack isn't true, so Cody already has at least one clue that he should retire it.

In order to prove something as true or false, you need at least a little bit of evidence. Barbara L. Fredrickson, PhD, a professor at the University of North Carolina, Chapel Hill, points out that "one scientifically tested way to stop this life-draining cycle is to dispute negative thinking. Dispute it the way a good lawyer would, by examining the facts."[5]

One of the fastest ways to get evidence is to get a second opinion. If a doctor gave you a serious diagnosis, you'd reach out to a second doctor to confirm what the first one said. When it comes to soundtracks, we're talking about the thoughts that shape our entire perception of life. It behooves us to ask someone if what we're thinking is true.

That's what Sal St. Germain, an electrical shop manager in Hawaii with the coolest name ever, did in the middle of a massive project at work. Of course he lives in Hawaii—you think he'd be living in Iowa with that name?

When I connected with him during the research for this book, he told me, "We had a project that was failing badly because we thought that we were constrained by some rules and regulations set forth by our parent organization."

Recognizing that they were stuck, Sal decided to ask his boss if what he and the team were believing was true. That was the easiest way to get some evidence. "My boss told us that we were actually the experts and that it was up to us to educate the people in our parent organization on how we conduct business."

Sal and his team had bad information. The mother ship wasn't holding them back; it was actually just the opposite. They were waiting for Sal to teach them what the best next move was. "That changed the mindset of the leaders in our group, and we were able to engage our parent org instead of feeling victimized by them." Changing their soundtrack turned the team from victims into partners. "As a result, we ended up implementing the change in record time and saved about $14 million over the next five years."

"Is it true?" is one of those questions that can help you change the culture of an entire business. Culture is just a collection of soundtracks playing consistently at a company. Sometimes they're selected on purpose. More often than not, they're accidental. The most common broken soundtrack in corporate America is "We need a meeting." Can you fathom the time, creativity, and productivity you'd save if you asked that soundtrack, "Is it true?"

Culture is just a collection of soundtracks playing consistently at a company.

Maybe you don't need a meeting. Maybe what's true is that you need an answer from one person on one issue. Instead of ten people wasting an hour kicking around ideas in a conference room together, all you need is a phone call, email, or one-on-one conversation with a decision maker. The next time a coworker trots out that old chestnut "We need a meeting," ask, "Is it true?" and then make sure that's really what they need.

Another popular soundtrack right now is that millennials are lazy and entitled. That one has been in vogue for years. If you want to defuse it and move in a different direction, when someone says that, ask, "Is it true?" Look for evidence. Is the person saying that ten millennials they've hired have all been lazy and entitled, or are they just repeating a popular thing said in the media? Are they responding to a Harvard Business School study about the decline in work ethic or mimicking something they heard a comedian say once?

Patrick Bradway, a pastor in Escanaba, Michigan, had a soundtrack that wasn't work-related but was every bit as frustrating. "For me it's finding a hobby, something to take my mind off of things. Ironically, I always think of what I should be doing instead. I have to clean the house and I need to focus on my wife and her needs. All good things, but I often just let myself get consumed and I never really allow myself to have a hobby because I think there are more pressing things I need to be doing."

That's an admirable approach to life. Patrick is saying that until he spends enough time with his wife, he can't have a hobby for himself. The problem is that there's no such thing as "enough." He'll never feel like he's cleaned the house enough or spent enough time with his wife.

I asked him what his wife would think if he found a new hobby and dedicated some time to it. His broken soundtrack was telling him, "You can't have a hobby because of your wife." His broken soundtrack told him she'd be furious at how selfish he was being. But is it true? Did he have evidence? Was his wife some hobby-ruining ogre? His answer didn't surprise me.

"My wife continually tells me to find a hobby. She always tells me to find friends to hang out with and go to a movie with."

She's eager for him to find a hobby, but the broken soundtrack is telling him just the opposite. Armed with new evidence, he's got a clear answer to the first question we ask our soundtracks.

Ask the thought behind the thought these questions

Tony Murtaugh popped open a full bottle of discount champagne and shook it all over Kris Luoto's parents' house on New Year's Eve one year.

As he showered the living room with bubbly, much to the horrified shouting of every other partygoer, I remember having two distinct thoughts:

1. He thinks he just won the NBA championship.
2. How did he get into this party?

No one really knew the answer to that question, which is always true of knuckleheads at parties. Someone probably invited Mike to the party. Mike told a friend about it. The friend told his cousin who owns a Jet Ski. Cousins own 72 percent of the Jet Skis in the country. The cousin then told Tony. The original invitee in these situations is rarely the problem. It's always the Tony behind the cousin behind the friend behind the Mike that causes all the ruckus.

The same principle is true of your broken soundtracks. Let's say you want to start a podcast. One of the first soundtracks you hear is, "I don't know how to do a podcast."

That's 100 percent true. You don't and admitting that is a great way to start learning what you need to do. But, a second soundtrack slips through the door behind that first one. It says, "It will be incredibly difficult to do a podcast." That might be 50 percent true. It won't be easy, but it's not going to be incredibly difficult either. Podcasting gets easier every day as the technology improves and more experts teach online classes.

The first two soundtracks aren't real issues, but there's a third lurking in the shadows. And "lurking" is the right word because as we discussed in chapter 1, overthinking has a tendency to skew negative.

Now, as you start to engage in the podcast and hit the kind of roadblocks you always hit when doing something new, you suddenly hear, "I'll never be able to do a podcast." Whoa, never? That's such a discouraging thing to think about a new challenge. How did that soundtrack get in here? That's zero percent true, and now you've got some rascal popping bottles of champagne all over Kris Luoto's mom's floral couch. (It was a lovely couch and teenage boys are unfortunately very bad at getting stains out of furniture.)

Knuckleheads and broken soundtracks tend to travel in bunches. As you retire the ones that are getting in the way by asking "Is it true?" and the next two questions, make sure you look at the thought behind the thought. It's the best way to make sure some uninvited guests haven't shown up at the party.

Question 2: Is it helpful?

The question "Is it true?" won't be enough to smoke out the lie in a broken soundtrack. That's why it's so annoying when someone tells you, "Stop overthinking that situation—it isn't true!" *Thanks, armchair Oprah. Your wisdom has changed my life.* It's not enough to just know something isn't true. Our soundtracks are much more tenacious than that, which is why we ask this second question.

Is the soundtrack you're listening to right now, the one that's on repeat, helpful? Does it move you forward or keep you stuck? Does it lead to a decision or limit a decision? Does it generate action or apathy?

Erin Zieren—no relation to Ian Ziering, but dang, that's close to *Sharknado* royalty—knows the power of this question.

49

She's an architect in Flowood, Mississippi, and like a lot of us, when a conversation with someone ends, the review process begins.

Did I say the right thing? Should I have said something different? Which parts of that conversation might be misinterpreted? When she said she didn't need my help, what did that mean? There was a little bit of conflict—should I resolve it with a phone call, email, or text? Does addressing it make the issue bigger or smaller? Is this a hill to die on or something I should overlook because we're friends?

Erin overthinks the whole situation, especially if there was any perceived friction. "I play the event over and over a thousand times and agonize how I should have reacted," she says. The path forward is obvious to her though: "Discussion with the person should be the first go-to, and it would solve things much easier."

That's one of the real costs of overthinking. It prevents us from taking the often simple steps that would alleviate the situation. Instead, Erin listens to a host of broken soundtracks. When I asked her how much time she wastes, she's quick to admit, "Days. I'm ashamed to say weeks in some complicated cases. To the point where it drives me mad; then I'm angry with myself for not biting the bullet and resolving it sooner."

If you asked that broken soundtrack if it was true, it might be able to trick you: "Sure, I'm helping you think through the situation. We're not obsessing, we're analyzing. I'm just preparing you for the next time." It could pretend to be true, which is why we always bring a second question to the table.

Is it helpful?

Do you think Erin would ever answer yes? Would she say that wasting days and even weeks feeling ashamed and angry at herself was helpful? Of course not. Think of what she could have done with that time instead.

Now multiply that problem across an entire company and imagine its implications on productivity.

Think about how many coworkers waste time, creativity, and productivity on soundtracks that aren't helpful instead of doing the simple things they know would fix the problem. What's that costing? Days? Weeks? Millions of dollars? That's not even hyperbole. Sal St. Germain's team in Hawaii saved $14 million when they stopped listening to a broken soundtrack.

How valuable will dealing with your broken soundtracks be?

Question 3: Is it kind?

Broken soundtracks are tricky and can often skate through the first two questions undetected. They're great at masquerading as the truth. How could they not be? You've been believing some of them for years. They're good at promoting themselves as helpful. Quick to call up examples of situations they've saved you from. But this last question is the one that will undo them.

Is it kind?

Is the soundtrack you're listening to kind to yourself? After you listen to it a few times, do you feel better about yourself? Are you encouraged about your life and your opportunities?

When Mike Peasley, PhD, and I asked more than ten thousand people how overthinking made them feel, 73 percent responded "inadequate." When asked if overthinking left them feeling drained, 52 percent of people said yes. Do you know why overthinking makes you feel inadequate and drained? Because you've been listening to unkind soundtracks about yourself on repeat.

Of the three questions we ask our soundtracks, this is definitely the one that is most likely to conjure up holding a sprig of sage and chanting in a friendship circle at a commune in Malibu. But pump the brakes for a second. No one is saying you have to get touchy-feely to send a soundtrack through this final filter. In fact, let's dip back into the world of science to really grasp why retiring unkind soundtracks matters.

Thirty years ago, Dr. Jon Kabat-Zinn, an MIT-trained professor from the University of Massachusetts Medical School, was one of the first scientists to study the health benefits of mindfulness. That's a popular word these days that invokes thoughts of candles, but Dr. Kabat-Zinn's definition of mindfulness is much more clinical and helpful to our discussion: "Mindfulness means paying attention in a particular way: on purpose, in the present moment, and nonjudgmentally."[6]

That last word is most important when it comes to weeding out unkind soundtracks. Kind soundtracks are nonjudgmental. Unkind soundtracks are judgmental. If your soundtrack is what a principal might tell you after you've been called into the office over the loudspeaker in the eighth grade, there's a chance it's not kind. If your soundtrack is what you're afraid people will find out about you someday—that is, you really don't have your life together—there's a chance it's not kind.

Google attempted to understand this problem on the team level when they launched Project Aristotle. They invested millions of dollars to understand what the most successful teams within the company had in common. They measured 180 different teams using over 35 different statistical models on hundreds of variables.[7] Probably would have been a lot faster to just google it, but if Google googles itself, our solar system will collapse inward.

Do you know what they found? "Google's data indicated that psychological safety, more than anything else, was critical to making a team work."[8] Psychological safety is a term Harvard Business School professor Amy Edmondson defines as a "shared belief held by members of a team that the team is safe for interpersonal risk-taking."[9] You can ask questions, suggest new ideas and admit you are wrong without being treated unkindly by the team. When you've got broken soundtracks firing shots at yourself all day, no wonder you get stuck. Your "team of one" isn't a safe place for growth or innovation.

The benefit of listening to kind soundtracks is bigger than you think. Those who have taken Kabat-Zinn's course, for instance, have been shown to experience less stress, less pain, reduced anxiety, clearer skin, and better immune functioning.[10] Clearer skin was the one that got me. I imagined Adam Levine from Maroon 5 in a skin care commercial for Proactiv saying, "Yeah, it wasn't the cream that helped me the most, it was that I stopped beating myself up so often."

When Herbert Benson, a Harvard physician, studied the effects of mindfulness on cardiovascular health, he discovered two things that had the greatest impact. The first was repeating a phrase—which is another way to say soundtrack—deliberately to yourself for a set period of time. The second key was gently bringing yourself back to the phrase by saying "Oh well" whenever you got distracted and thought about something else instead. The "Oh well" was an important part because it was a nonjudgmental, kind way to refocus.[11]

Resilience is allowing yourself to begin again when things don't go the way you expected the first time.

Instead of berating yourself with phrases like "I'm the worst at focusing" or "This will never work," all you do is say "Oh well" and begin again. We assume we have to be tougher than that and have the resilience of a Navy SEAL, but what is resilience other than allowing yourself to begin again when things don't go the way you expected the first time?

Whether the study was scientifically based or built from centuries-old religious practices, when it came to training yourself how to think, they all had one thing in common: kindness mattered. I couldn't find a single study that said, "The key to creating the thought life you want is to criticize yourself more often. The secret to getting better at anything is being harder on yourself."

Identifying soundtracks that aren't kind might feel like a fuzzy practice, but the benefits are clear and surprisingly practical. The first time I tried it, it improved every business trip I took far more than finally gaining access to the Delta Sky Club did.

No Room for Shame in the Suitcase

After years of repeating the soundtrack "I think I can be a public speaker" and then taking the actions to make it true, I started to get a lot more speaking engagements. I went from zero nights of business travel to about eighty nights a year. When I first started leaving for trips, I would make a big production about my exit for my kids. I'd express remorse that I was leaving, tell them how much I'd miss them, and say things like, "I'll be home in four sleeps." I acted like I was being deployed to the moon for a year and not embarking on a two-night stay at the DFW Courtyard Marriott. I should have just played Kansas's "Dust in the Wind" each time I packed my suitcase to put a chef's kiss on the whole scene.

Finally, one night my wife pulled me aside. "You're making the kids feel terrible about you being gone. You feel guilty about it, so you're exaggerating the experience and teaching them to be sad. They don't even know to be sad about this, but they'll reflect your emotions. So the sadder you act, the sadder they feel. We're not mad that you're traveling. We're not crushed. It's your job. Go do your job."

Jenny was right. Kids will respond to our emotions. The process involves *mirror neurons* in their brains that reflect what you put out as a parent. When my "good dads don't do business travel" soundtrack got loud, I felt sad and in turn taught my kids that they should feel sad too.

Perhaps worse than that, I was demonizing work. I was unknowingly teaching my kids that work was a terrible place that ripped you from your home and forced you to leave loved ones. We spend eighteen years teaching our kids that work sucks and then act surprised when they graduate from college and don't seem eager to get a job.

I'd never thought about it, but in the background of my life there were a few soundtracks playing that told me, "Good parents never travel for work" and "I should feel ashamed when I have to travel for work." Where did those come from? Well, my dad is a pastor and my mom is a dental hygienist, so I didn't grow up seeing parents travel for work. I thought, "I had good parents and they never traveled. Therefore, only bad parents travel." I'd accidentally believed those kinds of soundtracks for years, but now that they were out in the open, I could ask them the three questions.

Is it true? It is a little bit. I do sometimes feel sad leaving my kids for work, especially when there's a rare Nashville snow day and every dad on Instagram is posting a steady stream of photos from frolicking with their children with #MyKid WontNeedCounseling. I love being home, and there's definitely some truth to the idea that I feel sad leaving. At the same time, I also love the travel part of my job. I went to Disney twice in one week for two different events. The first one was at the Four Seasons with a room overlooking Cinderella's Castle. The second time was at a Marriott with a ten-person table in the dining room portion of my hotel room. I ate a cheeseburger from the food court at the head of the table like I was about to fire nine people over lunch. My travel is FUN.

Is it helpful? Maybe I should feel sad. Is that what a good dad feels—guilt about traveling? Is that soundtrack helping me be a better dad? Does it lead to me spending more time with my kids when I'm home? I could have spent a lot of time trying to figure that one out, but luckily I had a final question left in my arsenal.

Is it kind? To answer this one, I broke it down with the three parties involved:

1. *Is it kind to me?* Nope. Telling myself that I should feel ashamed every time I traveled wasn't kind. It ruined each trip and turned what could have been a fun experience into Shameapalooza. Public speaking is my favorite thing to do in the world. It wasn't kind that the minute after I received a new opportunity, a soundtrack told me I should feel bad about leaving home.

2. *Is it kind to my kids?* Nope. I was teaching them anxiety and stress. I might as well have sat them down and said, "Looks like you're having a pretty good day. Juice boxes, *Clifford the Big Red Dog*, favorite pajamas. I almost hate to do this. I need to let you know I'm leaving. I'll tell you that it's only for two nights, but because you have no real sense of how time works, that might seem like forever. It would mean a lot to me if you'd put a candle in the window each night until my safe return, for the road is perilous and I don't like my odds in the B boarding group of Southwest."

3. *Is it kind to my wife?* Nope. Three for three! Whipping my kids into an emotional mess right before I leave for a trip wasn't kind. "Now that I've got the kids crying, I'm going to bounce for a few days. Good luck with all of this."

The more I pulled the thread, the more obvious everything became. I decided to stop packing shame on my trips. I just didn't have room for it. Those old soundtracks were no longer invited on the trip. I started telling anyone who would listen that they should let go of it too. When other business travelers would bemoan their absence from home, I would encourage them that beating yourself up rarely accomplishes anything useful.

Always ask your soundtracks three questions:

1. Is it true?
2. Is it helpful?
3. Is it kind?

If you see me smiling someday even though I'm in the middle seat of a flight, you'll know why. Being kind to yourself is a secret weapon, and I use it every day.

Would You Say This to a Friend?

When you ask a broken soundtrack if it's true, helpful, and kind, it will often say, "Yes. This is for your own good. This is self-discipline. This is tough love." That soundtrack will try to disguise itself as a drill sergeant who is just trying to tear you down so that it can build you back up into a stronger, better version of yourself. You might not like it now, but one day you'll be glad you were this hard on yourself.

Nonsense.

A broken soundtrack will never transition into building you back up. It can't—that's not what it does. Take, for example, the soundtrack "You don't have enough time to finish everything today." Have you ever heard that one? First thing in the morning, as you scan your to-do list, you'll hear that soundtrack say that you're out of time. It will push the panic button, dumping loads of the stress hormone cortisol in your system until any shot at a peaceful, productive day is completely destroyed. Is it true? It might be. You don't have enough time to finish EVERYTHING. No one can finish everything in a single day. So yes, it's true—but is it kind?

That's where the lie starts to show.

For all the years you've been feeling behind on your to-do list, that soundtrack has never once told you, "Today is actually the day you have exactly the right amount of time you need. You've got the perfect amount—we did it!" It will never say that. If you're waiting for a broken soundtrack to turn into a kind soundtrack, quit waiting.

Broken soundtracks never evolve into new soundtracks on their own. That process is on us. We're in charge of retiring the old ones and replacing them with brand-new ones.

If you're still having trouble deciphering whether a soundtrack is kind, an easy way to check is to ask yourself, "If I repeatedly told a friend this, would they still want to be my friend?"

If I told my friend Wendy Maybury, a single mom superhero, that every time she travels for work she should be ashamed of herself, would she still want to be my friend? If I called her at the airport each time she was about to get on a plane and told her she was being a bad mom, would that be kind? Would she be excited to get my call, or would she quickly block my number whenever it came up?

If you wouldn't say it to a friend, there's a chance you shouldn't say it to yourself either.

Whatcha Gonna Do with All Them Thoughts?

Depending on who you read, thoughts are described in a variety of ways. I've heard it said that you should think about your thoughts like leaves floating down a river, cars on a highway, or clouds in the sky. You watch them pass by, an objective observer calmly picking out any that you don't want to have. "Oh, dear me, this thought isn't true, helpful, or kind. I shall remove it from the river of my life so the waters can flow more peacefully."

That sounds like a wonderful process. Alas, I have weapons-grade overthinking. It's persistent and evasive and tends to laugh at me when I try to shoo away errant soundtracks like unwelcome leaves in the river of Jon.

Some days I find a thousand untrue, unhelpful, unkind thoughts on my shore. Other days I find the same thought I swore I retired yesterday rushing by again and gathering an ungodly amount of frequent-floater miles. Fortunately, there is one thing you can do that will stop all your overthinking forever.

3. Turn Down the Dial

I wish the last sentence of chapter 2 was true, don't you?

Wouldn't it be amazing if I had one thing you could do that would stop all your overthinking forever?

All your friends would say, "What's different about you? You seem more calm, confident, and successful. Have you been drinking a lot of water?"

"Thank you for noticing, but no, it's not water. It's Jon Acuff. He told me the cure to ending overthinking. I'd share it, but you should buy the book yourself so his kids can go to college."

Wow, I wasn't expecting that. My oldest daughter's high school English teacher told her to just find a free PDF of *Lord of the Flies* online instead of buying the book or to get a bootleg copy of the audiobook on YouTube. That you're telling people to pay for art is truly encouraging.

Art is exactly what it would be, this perfect cure. It would be a miracle. My singular masterpiece. It wouldn't stay singular for long, of course, because if it was successful, I would immediately release a follow-up book to capitalize on my newfound fame. That one would be called *The Second Cure*, or

Cure-ier, and I'd be on the cover of that one with a wry grin that seemed to say, "I can't believe I found another cure for overthinking either!"

I spent decades looking for that one thing that would end my overthinking forever. I'm a sucker for motivational gurus, and the bigger the overpromise, the bigger my belief that this one would be the one that worked. I was convinced I was only one idea, one technique, one hack away from changing everything all at once.

I was wrong.

No matter what I tried, no matter how long I held my breath, no matter what I studied, I couldn't completely turn off my broken soundtracks. You know you're a bit stuck when you try to play your meditation app at 2× speed. It worked for audiobooks. Maybe if I got twice as much mindfulness in half as much time, everything would be fixed. Despite my best efforts, my broken soundtracks still kept getting loud sometimes. I kept retiring them, assuming they'd be gone forever. But then they'd pop up in unexpected moments, like Brett Favre refusing to leave the NFL for good. I felt like a failure until I had breakfast with David Thomas.

It's a Dial

David Thomas wears cool glasses. That's not the most important thing about him, but it is distinct. He's one of those guys who can wear glasses with clear frames without looking like he's a dad still trying to pull off Air Jordans. "What, these? Didn't mean to flex." In addition to his excellent ocular fashion sense, he's also the director of family counseling at Daystar, a center for kids in Nashville. He's the author of six books and an accomplished public speaker, but it was an offhand comment he made over coffee that changed what I believed about retiring broken soundtracks.

In the middle of a long list of questions I was asking him, David said, "The problem with the internal voices we hear is that we want a switch." I hadn't heard thoughts described that way, so I asked him to explain what he meant.

"We think that there's a switch out there and if we can just find it, we can turn off the background noise completely. We only have to do it one time and we'll never hear it again. People want there to be a switch."

"Those people are crazy," I replied, having spent the last few years of my life looking for that exact thing.

"It's not a switch though," he continued, "it's a dial. The goal isn't to turn it off forever, the goal is to turn down the volume. It's going to get louder sometimes. That's how dials work. But when life turns up the negative thoughts, we get to turn them down. That takes a lot of the pressure off because when you hear one again, it's not a sign that you've failed to shut it off and need to go find a different switch. It's just time for an action that will turn it back down."

I wanted to jump on top of the table in the diner and shout, "It's a dial! It's a dial!" and then throw a sixpence to a street urchin like I was Ebenezer Scrooge so he could buy his family a fat Christmas goose.

When you live with a switch mentality, you set yourself up for automatic failure because it triggers the perfectionism soundtrack. It goes something like this: You hear a soundtrack that says, "If you could find the switch, you could turn it off and never be bothered by broken soundtracks again. You're just one book, one exercise, one diet away from never hearing negative thoughts." The switch can be any positive thing that you believe will deliver instant, forever silence from a broken soundtrack.

That's when the perfectionism soundtrack gets louder. "Perfection is possible! The switch is the answer!" That's an amazing promise. Who doesn't want to believe that? So you try the new thing and it works for a while. The breathing technique relaxes you. The book offers fantastic insights. The counseling session encourages you. But then a week later, a month later, a day later, depending on how strong a particular broken soundtrack is, you hear it again.

Oh no! It wasn't perfect. It's still playing. The switch failed. Perfectionism will never tell you that it's the switch's fault. It's always your fault. It does this because then you'll start looking for a new switch instead of questioning the whole process. Time to find a second switch. You read a different book, try a different diet, change jobs, change cities, change spouses. That's what it's like to live with a switch mentality.

A dial is just the opposite. A dial approach says, "The goal isn't to stop listening forever to all my broken soundtracks. The goal is to turn them down when they get loud. The goal is to head them off at the pass when a traffic jam, unexpected corporate merger, call from an estranged sibling, or any of the billion surprises life throws at you cranks the volume to 10."

Retiring broken soundtracks is a patient practice, not a singular event. Some days you won't hear any broken soundtracks at all. Other days you'll look up and realize one snuck back into your life when you weren't paying attention. When that happens, you have to turn the dial down.

What It Takes to Develop a Few Turn-Down Techniques

You have two options when it comes to life: manicure your world so perfectly that nothing ever threatens to turn the volume up on a broken soundtrack, or learn a few healthy ways to turn the dial down when it gets loud.

In the first approach, you have to avoid every idiot online, rain, taxes, long wait times at restaurants, people who are slow getting off airplanes, unexpected global pandemics, and Carol from accounting. This is very time-consuming and, I'm afraid to say, impossible.

In the second approach, you learn a few techniques that you keep in your back pocket and use to turn down the volume before it gets too loud. This approach is a lot more fun and actually possible. That's the one David Thomas challenged me on there in that diner.

"What are the techniques?" I asked him, taking notes as fast as I could and hoping he would give me four or five very specific things to do. (I was still looking for switches at this point.)

David explained, "They're different for every person based on how they're wired, but essentially they're a handful of actions you take in moments when the music gets too loud. For instance, for some people, they'll list petting a dog as one because it's been proven to release serotonin. I always tell people to make a few of them physical. We're trying to move the blood back from the dinosaur part of your brain to the thinking part, and movement helps. They shouldn't involve screens at first; they should be easy, accessible, and extend beyond one context."

The reason they should be easy is that broken soundtracks love complicating things because then there's lots of fodder for overthinking. Let's pretend that one of my broken soundtracks is that I'll never be able to write another book. Let's imagine for a second that every time I sit down to write, that soundtrack tries to fire up and tell me I'm out of words, every good book has already been written, and everyone already knows the ideas I think are so new. Hypothetically.

Maybe one of my techniques is that when I hear that soundtrack, I turn it down by writing in my favorite seat in my favorite coffee shop at my favorite time of day. That sounds great on the surface, but what happens when I show up one day and someone is in my seat? I know exactly what happens because here's the conversation I've had a dozen times:

Soundtrack: Someone is sitting in our seat.

Me: It's not a big deal.

Soundtrack: Are you kidding me right now? It's the biggest deal of all the deals that have ever been. That spot is perfect. The table is small enough that you don't feel bad about hogging a big table by yourself, but it's big enough that you still have room to spread out your stuff.

Me: Like a Goldilocks table.

Soundtrack: Exactly. And the lighting is perfect. It's bright enough to get some work done but also moody enough that you feel like you're a character in a movie who is going through some stuff but is going to make it. That table is also an adequate distance from the children's room, which means with noise-canceling headphones you can barely hear them. I demand we get some very private work done in this very public place.

Me: I think it's going to be okay.

Soundtrack: How about you leave the thinking to me. What you're not seeing is that our only option is to sit near phone-call guy, the one person here who feels empowered to have loud conference calls like he's in WeWork and not a coffee shop. "I DON'T KNOW, GREG! I RAN THE NUMBERS AND I DON'T THINK THE CLIENT IS GOING TO GO FOR THIS NEW BUDGET!" This is a nightmare. I can't believe someone is in our spot.

Me: It's not technically my spot. I don't own it.

Soundtrack: Not with that attitude you don't. Let's just go home. None of the work you do outside of your spot is going to be good anyway. Let's call it a wrap. This day is over. P.S.: You'll probably never write another book.

Me: It's only 7 a.m.

Soundtrack: Life comes at you fast.

I wish that conversation was even a little bit exaggerated, but I promise you it's not. "Writing in my favorite seat in my favorite coffee shop at my favorite time of day" might seem like a good turn-down technique I can use when I'm stuck with my writing, but it's not. In fact, it's just the opposite. It's a broken soundtrack in disguise. It's too rigid. There are too many rules. It leads to more inaction instead of action, which is always the sign of a broken soundtrack.

I need to be able to use my turn-down techniques easily and in a variety of situations. Taking your dog on a walk is a great way to distract yourself from overthinking, but not if you're at work. That's why you need techniques for more than just one context.

Armed with a little information and excited to explore the dial concept, I decided to see if other people were already using their own turn-down techniques. I immediately ran into a tangle of disclaimers.

A Disclaimer about Disclaimers

During the research process for this book, I asked thousands of people what techniques they use to deal with overthinking. Online, in surveys, on phone calls, at dinner parties, in Ubers, I peppered people with questions.

I was surprised by two things:

1. More people use turn-down techniques than I previously suspected.
2. Nobody talks about them.

In conversations, people would lower their voices and say, "Well, I know this is silly, but . . ." and then they'd tell me about something they'd been doing every morning for the last year. For example, Adam Dupuis, a loan administration manager from Greensboro, North Carolina, told me he says "thank you" the minute his feet hit the ground and then at night before he falls asleep. When he described the benefits, he said, "This sounds totally hokey, but it's been a great way to start and end my day."

"Cheesy," "weird," and "dumb" were also words I heard a lot. Even if the technique had changed someone's life, there was a real temptation to begin the conversation with a disclaimer. People were afraid of being judged a certain way, so they prejudged themselves before you had a chance to.

That's unfortunate because it means the best music doesn't really have a chance to go viral. We'll share our broken soundtracks, lament online about all the things that aren't working for us in life, safe in the knowledge that no one will ever really judge us for those. But when it comes to the good stuff, the music that's making each day easier and brighter, we hold that close to the vest.

As you do the activities inside this book, you'll be tempted to use your own disclaimers with yourself. How do I know? Well, have you ever had an idea and then determined it wouldn't work, even before you wrote it down? As in, the idea didn't even make it to a piece of paper or a note in your phone before you self-edited it? You should be nodding your head right now, because everyone has done that.

That's a broken soundtrack because every idea is worthy of at least being captured. There are tens of millions of ideas that die early deaths every day because people tell themselves, "That's weird, that's silly, that's cheesy, that will never work." It's staggering to think of the works of art, business innovations, and cures for disease that we've lost because someone prejudged an idea before it had a chance to really grow.

Don't do that today. Explore what works for you without making disclaimers. Don't judge a turn-down technique before you test it in your own life.

Turn Down for What? My Five Favorite Techniques

I tried dozens of different turn-down techniques after David Thomas explained the dial idea to me. I read stacks of books. I took online courses. I started and stopped new sports. Over the years, these are the five techniques that have helped me the most when my broken soundtracks have tried to get loud again.

1. Running

I need endorphins like fish need water. When I got serious about working on my overthinking, I got more serious about running. A few miles alone does wonders for my head and my heart. I don't get to do it every day, but if I go three or four days without getting at least a little bit of exercise, my broken soundtracks get a lot louder.

If you hate running, that's awesome. I hate cycling, but some people love it. I don't like the clothes you have to wear, and I'm not a fan of any sport that occasionally involves getting hit by a car. My friend Randy got hit three different times before his parents had an intervention and bought him a mountain bike. I've also never had to change a flat tire on my running shoes. I wish I had discovered my distaste for cycling before I purchased a $2,000 carbon fiber road bike built for climbing the French Alps, but I have a real penchant for making expensive mistakes that hang on my garage wall and shame me for six months. I waited another six months to sell the bike back to the store I bought it from, because a broken soundtrack told me all the employees would think I was a failure.

Don't ever use any form of exercise you hate as a turn-down technique, but find your own way to get some endorphins into your system.

2. LEGO Sets

I stumbled on this one completely by accident. One Christmas, I gave my kids the LEGO Harry Potter Hogwarts Castle. It's a 6,020-piece ode to nerd-dom, complete with Hagrid's hut, Harry's dragon (from the fourth book, which is clearly the best), and even Dolores Umbridge's pink office. We didn't speed through it, but instead built it a bag or two a day, taking our time and watching it come together. There was something peaceful about seeing real progress. Most of my work is mental and I never see the results. There also aren't any instructions for my career. What are the steps for becoming a full-time writer and speaker? I find following the LEGO instructions really satisfying.

3. Lists

During busy seasons, I often hear the soundtrack "You've got too much to do and not nearly enough time to do it all."

I feel overwhelmed because I don't know which seemingly important task to focus on first. I turn the dial down on that soundtrack with a list. A list is the fastest way to bring clarity to chaos. Sometimes I create a list for that specific moment. Listing out what I need to get done on a project puts everything into perspective. Sometimes the list is designed to bring peace to a repetitive activity like packing for a trip. I've used the same packing list for the last five years. Sometimes the list centers on what I need to accomplish on a certain day.

> **A list is the fastest way to bring clarity to chaos.**

During a busy travel season, I found myself writing down five to ten things every morning that I needed to accomplish that day on the notepads hotels keep on nightstands. Because they were small, I couldn't do what I usually do, which is completely overthink my to-do list, adding a hundred tasks until I'd need a 96-hour Tuesday to accomplish it all. The boundary of the paper worked so well that I decided to start doing that at home too. I remembered that author James Altucher uses old-school waitress pads to capture new ideas, so I ordered a stack. Will it work? I don't know yet, but testing techniques gives you the creative freedom to try out as many options as you want.

I don't have fifty lists, but at any given time I have three or four that I'm actively using to turn the volume down. Putting one together is peaceful for me. Crossing the items off is peaceful for me. Tweaking the list to make it even more useful next time is peaceful for me. If your broken soundtracks ever feel chaotic, try making a list of what you need to do. Overthinking will hate that in the best possible way.

4. Minor tasks, massive payoff

When I want to turn the volume down, I put my laundry away. I go to the mailbox. I rake the yard. I fill up my oldest daughter's car with gas. I clean my desk. I clear the stairs of the items that have been placed there by my wife in the hope that someone, anyone, will finally admit they are there and put them away. A great way to get out of your head and into your world is to do a task you can actually finish.

That's why you'll see me at the grocery store some afternoons buying a single item. We weren't desperately out of Salt & Vinegar Pringles, though they are clearly the best variety, but I needed an achievable task to help me get unstuck from a bit of overthinking. Those might all seem like menial tasks, but the dividend they pay when it comes to turning down the volume is massive.

5. Friends

When I find myself in the middle of a broken soundtrack, one of the fastest ways to turn it down is to talk to a friend over coffee. That might seem intimidating at first, but don't believe the lie that tells you you're the only one who has broken soundtracks. As I mentioned, when I surveyed more than ten thousand people, 99.5 percent of them said they struggle with overthinking. We all overthink.

When you tell a friend a broken soundtrack, two things happen:

1. They say it's not true.
2. They share one of their own.

When you tell a friend a **broken soundtrack**, two things happen:

1. They say it's **not true**.

2. They **share** one of their own.

Why will they tell you it's not true? Because the easiest lies to see through are someone else's. The easiest music to hear accurately is someone else's. When friends tell me a soundtrack that's being a jerk to them, I tell them the truth. "You're not the worst mom in the world. No, that was probably Hitler's mom." See how easy that was for me? And then I'd tell you one of my soundtracks, because that's always what happens when good friends get together.

Is That Really All You've Got?

What kind of self-respecting overthinker shares a list with only five items on it? I mean, really, what if you hate LEGO? You ever step on one? That's the devil's carpet. What if running feels like a form of punishment? I might as well have said, "Flossing your teeth is a good turn-down technique." What if all your friends have wispy mustaches and are going to tell you that you should definitely get that face tattoo with "mizunderstood" spelled with an intentional z to highlight how different you are from conventional society? What then?

We're overthinkers. We don't believe in lists that are five items long. We roll fifty strong or we don't roll at all!

I agree.

50 Turn-Down Techniques You Can Use Today When Your Broken Soundtracks Get Loud

1. Go for a short drive down one of your favorite roads with the windows down and the music up. (I just wrote a Bruce Springsteen song.)
2. Drink a cup of coffee. Caffeine is the nectar of the gods.
3. Clean a drawer—or a whole closet if you've got the time.
4. Google "Steven Seagal" and "Russia" and see what he's been up to lately. You will not be disappointed.
5. Put something back where it belongs. The shoes in my house always seem to be on adventures far from their home in the garage.
6. Take your dog for a walk or even to the dog park. I've been told it's creepy to go to the dog park to pet all the dogs if you don't own one. Noted.
7. Watch fifteen minutes of a British baking show where the judges encourage contestants instead of shaming them on a deeply personal level for their icing choices.
8. Knit a few rows on your turn-down scarf.
9. Take a nap. Remember those things you raged against in childhood? Now we love them.
10. Write a thank-you note to someone using actual paper and actual stamps and your actual hand.

11. Text something encouraging to a friend if that last one felt altogether too exhausting.

12. Add a few pieces to a puzzle.

13. Read a bit of fiction. Don't force yourself through the classics if you despise them. Grab a beach book, where every single chapter has a climax and the main character's name is something dramatic like Jackson Steelsmith or Savannah Orion.

14. Use a meditation app like Headspace or Calm for ten minutes.

15. Teach your toddler how to put on shoes. Just kidding. Why would you do that to yourself? Buy a pair of Crocs for them and then call it a day. Nobody has time for laces.

16. Go to the gym. If you're not motivated, sign up for a class that costs you money so you've got some skin in the game.

17. If you don't have access to the gym, do ten jumping jacks, ten push-ups, or ten sit-ups.

18. If those are your three least-favorite things to do, go for a short walk.

19. Swing on a playground for ten minutes. Somewhere along the way to adulthood most of us lost touch with that simple joy.

20. Pretend to be your favorite professor and hold class outside for yourself today. Find a bench at work or a chair in your backyard and get some fresh air.

21. Watch ten minutes of your favorite comedian.

22. Take a bath or shower. Try real shampoo, not just a spritz of dry shampoo, a deception I caught my

wife using after fifteen years of marriage. Just when you think you know someone.

23. Take a few deep breaths. The nice thing about this one is you were probably already planning to breathe today, so you might as well make a few of them deep.

24. Listen to your favorite music, even if it's the wrong season. You want to bust out the *Charlie Brown Christmas* soundtrack in July? Go for it.

25. Call your mom.

26. Or, equally helpful, depending on your relation-ship with your mom, give yourself a week off from talking to your mom.

27. Dress up. I know the American dream is to work from home in your pajamas, but tired sweatpants are the uniform of broken soundtracks. Flan-nel feels like failure after a few hours. A robe is clothes melatonin. That's one of the things we all learned working from home during the corona-virus pandemic. Put on a belt and you'll already feel like you have a little bit of momentum.

28. Catch up on the latest episode of a podcast you love.

29. Look through your camera roll at the photos of your last vacation. David Thomas said that once you've got a few physical turn-down techniques, it's great to add some digital ones too.

30. Plan your next vacation. Pick a place, pick a time of year, and pick one activity you'll do when you go there.

31. Watch one of your favorite movies from the 1980s or 1990s. Start with *Aspen Extreme*, which

the *Seattle Times* rightfully called "*Top Gun* on the Ski Slopes."

32. Light a candle or diffuse essential oils if you're at home and won't have to talk to HR about all the fires.

33. Start a new hobby. Learn to play guitar (start with "Wonderwall" by Oasis, obviously). Try watercolor painting. Sign up for a pottery class.

34. Balance your personal budget. This one would give me a panic attack, but for a lot of people, dealing with numbers is a great way to quiet down all the emotions broken soundtracks add to situations.

35. Build a "bliss box" with a few of your favorite items that always put you in a good mood.

36. Get a bird feeder. In a matter of days, you'll be amazed at the flying art that's visiting your backyard.

37. Yell at squirrels. You get to do this one for free if you get a bird feeder.

38. Spend a few minutes with an adult coloring book. That sounds like maybe Cinemax has a coloring book series, but they're actually an incredibly popular craft that a lot of adults enjoy doing.

39. Play any game except Monopoly with your kid. You don't have nine hours to turn down this soundtrack.

40. Eat a small snack. Snickers is right, you're not you when you're hungry.

41. Get a haircut, get your nails done, or get a massage. This is 100 percent the "treat yo'self" collection of actions.

42. Spend a few minutes scrolling through a few of your favorite Instagram accounts.

43. Play your favorite game. If you're at home, knock out a few minutes of *Fortnite* or *Smash Bros*. If you're on your lunch break at work, open up an app and grow some virtual corn.

44. Watch clips of underdogs auditioning for singing shows and wowing the judges.

45. Speaking of clips, watch members of the military returning home to surprise their kids. Just get ready to explain to a coworker why you're sobbing at your desk.

46. Get out in the woods. You don't have to hike the Appalachian Trail tomorrow, but a stroll through the forest is a great way to reset the day.

47. Write it out. Don't let the broken soundtracks just spin in your head. Shrink them down to size by putting them on a piece of paper.

48. Do something nice for someone else. Get a friend flowers, take a coworker to the airport, buy coffee for a neighbor, etc.

49. Create a playlist of your favorite chill-out or GET-UP songs. The first might be full of Danish ambient composers who make entire albums of what the lonely streets of Copenhagen sound like at night. The second might be full of what it would sound like if *The Fast and the Furious 27* was filmed in Copenhagen.

50. Take a break from your phone if any of your broken soundtracks are connected to how much time you're spending on it.

If you can't find a turn-down technique on that list that works for you, then here's #51: "Stop lying." I know you didn't already try the Steven Seagal Russia idea, which NOBODY saw coming. Putin named him as a special envoy to America? What does that even mean?

If you do something different though, let me know. Post your favorite turn-down technique on Instagram with #soundtracks and tag me @JonAcuff so I see it. I'm always looking for fresh ways to turn down my soundtracks and would love to see what you're up to.

Retiring broken soundtracks is a fun way to start dealing with over-thinking. If you do that, you'll be miles ahead of 99 percent of the people on the planet who never think about what they think.

> Post your favorite turn-down technique on Instagram with #soundtracks and tag me @JonAcuff so I see it.

But the real fun is when you learn to replace your soundtracks with music you actually want to listen to.

4. Borrow from the Best

The question isn't whether or not you'll hear a soundtrack today. The question is whether you'll choose it or chance it.

Some mornings, I forget this. I wake up and before I even turn the light on I say, "Okay, feelings, what soundtrack do you want to listen to today?" My feelings say, "The angry one!" I don't usually ask why they've picked this particular tune. I don't question if someone attacked us during the night that I have forgotten about. I just say, "It's a deal!" I jump out of bed with Rage Against the Suburb blasting at an 11.

"Why are you so angry?" my wife will ask.

"No idea!" I say, a storm cloud of completely unprovoked frustration barreling through the kitchen.

Has that ever happened to you? Before your feet hit the floor, your feelings have picked an angry soundtrack to listen to all day. I know it has because we have a phrase for it: "I woke up on the wrong side of the bed."

I would love to have a better day, but my feelings decided this morning that today would suck. It's really my bed, you see. One side is pleasant, the other side is where I keep my pit vipers—and alas, it is on this side that I have risen.

> When you don't choose a soundtrack to listen to, the music doesn't stop. You just hear a bunch of songs you don't like.

I like feelings. This isn't where I'm going to tell you that feelings are useless or stupid or out to get you. Feelings and Netflix are two of the things that separate us from the animals. But as I started putting my overthinking under the microscope, I began to realize that feelings aren't the best DJ.

One morning I woke up and my feelings said, "Today's soundtrack is stress. That's what we're listening to all day."

This time I actually said, "Why?"

My feelings responded, "Because you sent that big proposal to the client and they might not accept it."

That felt true. It didn't feel particularly helpful or kind to myself to be stressed out, but it was a big proposal, so I rolled with that soundtrack. I wish I could compartmentalize better. I tried, I promise. I told my overthinking, "Hey, let's not stress until we get that email from the client this afternoon. I have a lot of other work to do this morning that doesn't involve that proposal at all." My overthinking giggled and then proceeded to play the stress soundtrack in the background of my entire day.

Birds can fly across the Atlantic Ocean without stopping because they can sleep with only half their brain while the other half stays in motion. That's what it feels like when I'm distracted by overthinking. I went through the whole day, but half my brain was playing that soundtrack at full volume. *What if the client doesn't accept my proposal? What if they want to cut it in half? What if the whole thing falls apart?* I listened to thoughts like that on repeat for hours. I couldn't focus on my kids. I couldn't pay attention to my wife. I was mostly absent from meetings. I was too busy attending a private concert for one.

At the end of the day I got a message from the client. Not only did they accept the proposal, they wanted to double the amount of work, which meant doubling the amount of money they were going to pay me. It was the biggest contract of my entire life. I shouted for joy in my garage when I read the email. The stress soundtrack had to end now, right?

The next morning, I woke up and my feelings said, "Today's soundtrack is stress. That's what we're listening to all day."

I said, "Wait, what? I understand why we listened to the stress soundtrack yesterday. We were worried about the proposal, but it worked out! It's a huge win. We should listen to a celebration soundtrack!"

And my feelings said, "Sure, you got a massive deal, but what if you can't deliver? A deal that size brings a lot of pressure."

That was the moment I realized that no matter how my circumstances changed during the course of a day, my feelings weren't always going to pick a soundtrack that accurately matched what was

> **You're better at picking out great thoughts to listen to than your feelings are.**

really going on. If stress was the song of the day, there wasn't a single event that could change that tune. If doubt was the music my feelings set in motion, then all the wins in the world wouldn't do anything.

I decided that maybe I should be the one to pick the soundtrack. Maybe I could make my own playlist and listen to that instead. I didn't know how to do that yet, but it had to be better than just pressing shuffle and accepting whatever soundtrack my feelings served up.

Start Your Playlist with Somebody Else's Song

One night my wife and I went out to dinner with another couple from Nashville. We didn't know each other very well, so while we waited for our food, we asked the type of wide-sweeping questions you ask in moments like that: "How did you two meet?" "What brought you to Nashville?" "What are your hobbies?"

I piped up to that last one and admitted, "This is kind of silly, but I love graphic novels." The table got oddly quiet and my wife leapt into the silence. "He means comic books. That's what a graphic novel is, it's a comic book." It didn't hit me that when you say "graphic novel" most people who actually went to the prom assume that means erotica. They don't think *Batman*, they think *50 Shades of Grey*.

There I was at dinner with near strangers, proudly declaring that one of my favorite hobbies was erotica. "A lot of people say they like it for the stories and the plot, but not me. I'm a big fan of the graphicness." That was an awkward night, but I'm no stranger to conversational car wrecks. I certainly encountered a lot of them when I talked to people about the topic of overthinking.

When I would tell someone I was writing about overthinking, they would inevitably say, "Oh, I need that book. I'm an overthinker."

I'd ask, "What do you overthink?" and they'd reply, "Everything!" I would get them to list out a few areas of their life where overthinking was a particularly big hassle and then offer a few suggestions for turning down those soundtracks. But if I then switched gears and asked, "What soundtracks would you like to listen to instead?" I would be met with blank stares.

I might as well have said, "I love porn! Please pass the salt."

It was 100 percent easier for people to list out broken soundtracks they wanted to retire than it was to list out the new soundtracks they wanted to jam. The same thing happened to me in 2008. When I decided to listen to the soundtrack "I think I can be a public speaker and author," I didn't spend the next few days writing down other positive thoughts I wanted to listen to.

That's not how it happened at all. The blank paper was too intimidating for me. So, instead of trying to come up with my own, I did something unusual: I listened to somebody else's soundtrack.

God Bless Dorothy Parker

I borrowed a soundtrack from author Dorothy Parker fifteen years ago and haven't looked back once. I've used it almost every day of my life since. It's one of those true-north soundtracks that guides my books, my career, and my research. Now that I've built it up to the point that you'll definitely be underwhelmed, allow me to share it.

Parker once said, "Creativity is a wild mind and a disciplined eye."

The wild mind means you give yourself permission to put a thousand different ideas in your head. You notice a song lyric, a comment from the mailman, a sign at a coffee shop, a question your curious toddler asked, and an article in the *New York Times*. You collect anything that is remotely interesting to you.

Then you look at that vast collection of unrelated ideas and have the discipline to see the connection between them in a way no one has before. I use this approach to write books, articles, and speeches. For example, one of the topics I talk about a lot to companies is empathy. In my speech, I share a story a chimney sweep told me in Branson, Missouri, a marketing principle I learned working for Bose, and a rap lyric from Dr. Dre. Those three ideas had nothing to do with each other when I initially collected them, but when I connected them they turned into a highly memorable soundtrack for audiences.

When I woke up to the fact that I could choose my own soundtracks, I made an important decision. I didn't have time to wait for a list of eureka moments to show up. The lightning strike of "I think I can be a public speaker and author" took me thirty-two years to have. I didn't want to be sixty-four and saying, "Okay, I've figured out a second soundtrack that I think is true, helpful, and kind for my life."

I'd turned down my overthinking a bit with the dial approach, but I felt like my best shot at long-term success was to turn up some new music. And the antidote to overthinking isn't more thinking—the antidote is action.

You don't think your way out of overthinking. You act your way out. You retire broken soundtracks. You replace them with new ones. You repeat those so often they become as automatic as the old ones. Those are all actions.

I decided that instead of doing a deep dive into my own head to find a new soundtrack, I'd look around for one. I liked the odds of that a lot better because it gave me access to the songs seven billion other people were listening to instead of just my own. I decided to be like Dorothy Parker. I'd have a wild mind. I'd collect stories and comments from friends and movie quotes and anything else that lit me up. Then I'd have the eye discipline to see the connection and remix it until I had a playlist that made me unstoppable every morning.

How can I say this with such confidence?

Because my life is dope.

What Would Kanye Do?

When you give your brain permission to start finding new soundtracks for your collection, you'll be surprised how many phrases jump out at you in the most unexpected places. It's practically impossible to ignore them. That's how a long-forgotten video clip about Kanye West yielded a fresh soundtrack for me.

In the clip, comedian Dave Chapelle tells *Tonight Show* host Jimmy Fallon about the first time he met Kanye. Although Kanye was relatively unknown at the time, Chapelle had

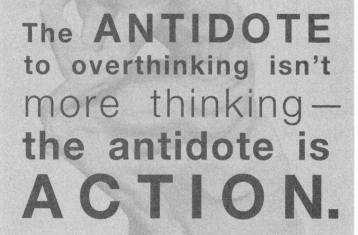

The **ANTIDOTE** to overthinking isn't more thinking — the antidote is **ACTION.**

booked the young artist to perform on his Comedy Central show. They were together watching clips of the show that hadn't been aired yet, like the famous Rick James skit. In the middle of that moment, Kanye's phone rang, and Chapelle told Fallon, "This is when everyone knew Kanye was going to be a star."

On the phone, Kanye told the caller, "No, no I can't. Because I'm at the edit for *The Dave Chapelle Show* watching sketches that no one has seen before." Then he paused and said, "Because my life is dope and I do dope *#$@." Then he hung up. Fallon burst to his feet at the telling of the story. Chappelle said, "No record out, he didn't even have a record out!"[1]

Kanye's confidence, enthusiasm, and willingness to accept how fun his life was jumped out at me. What if I could hear that soundtrack every time something good happens? "My life is dope and I do dope *#$@." It would sure beat what I usually hear, which is, "Must be nice."

I don't know where that one started, but I envision an old woman wearing spectacles looking down on me and criticizing whatever smidgen of joy I've just experienced.

Must be nice to get a book deal.

Must be nice to set your own schedule.

Must be nice to be able to afford that vacation.

It's probably cousins with the phrase "Somebody has a lot of free time!" If anyone ever says this to you, they're saying, "I'm a lot busier than you and thus more important." Only you can't say that in real life, so instead people say things like "Must be nice" and "Somebody has a lot of free time!"

The internet factors in here too. I once posted a photo of my alarm clock. I was up at 4:30 a.m. for a flight and asked my followers what they were doing up so early. One person responded, "I'm looking at your clock thinking that it *must be nice* to call 4:30 early. My daily is 3:50 a.m., and if I overslept to 4:30 I would be upset."

Joke's on him, because Mark Wahlberg would be disappointed in both of us for missing a 2 a.m. burpee session with the Rock. We're both lazy in that story.

I liked Kanye's soundtrack and decided to borrow it. The next time something good happened to me, I said out loud, "My life is dope." I didn't say the second part, because I've got young kids with big ears and they're already reeling from the fact that their dad is into graphic novels.

It felt strange to say "My life is dope" the first ten or twenty times, but then something funny happened: I discovered gratitude. Everyone always talks about how important it is to be grateful, but I could never connect with that idea because I had too many broken soundtracks in the way.

> "My life is dope."
> —Kanye West

You can't have gratitude if you can't first admit something is good. Whenever I tried to, I'd hear soundtracks like "Must be nice," which was guilt that I didn't deserve something, or "Don't get your hopes up," which was fear that I'd lose the good thing if I enjoyed it too much. I didn't write down the Kanye soundtrack "My life is dope" thinking that it'd lead me to a lesson in gratitude. I wrote it down because I thought it was funny, ridiculous, and inspiring. Then, when I put it into action, I learned something unexpected: there was gratitude on the other side of it.

That's what's so fascinating about replacing your broken soundtracks with new ones. It always leads to places you can't imagine. Recognizing that, I started borrowing soundtracks from everywhere.

One afternoon, I told my Lyft driver I was working on a book but it was a hard project. He said, "Nothing good is ever easy." I wrote that down.

I did an event with musician Andy Gullahorn. He's really into badminton. I told him I'd love to play but hadn't before, so I wouldn't be very good. He said, "No one is good at things they've never done before." I wrote that down.

I read a book by Deena Kastor, the female American record holder for the marathon. After a successful career, she was burned out on the sport of running and almost quit. Instead, she hired legendary running coach Joe Vigil and learned a completely different approach. He taught her that "shaping her mind to be more encouraging, kind and resilient could make her faster than she'd ever imagined possible."[2]

That switch in her thinking and training helped her win America's first marathon Olympic medal in twenty years. One of her soundtracks when things get tough is a question: "Are you going to throw in the towel finally, or are you gonna drop that hammer?"[3] I wrote that down.

Crispin Porter Bogusky, an ad agency behind massive campaigns like Burger King's "The King," thinks positivity is so important that they list it as one of their secrets to good work in their employee handbook. They call it *delusional positivity*. They believe that "there is no way we could do what we do here without a relentlessly positive attitude. It shapes our future.

It creates our momentum. It keeps us moving forward when we're pushing the boundaries of possibility."

That's a lot to swallow, especially in an industry like advertising where it's easy to become jaded and cynical. They're aware of that and chose "delusional" on purpose. "The 'delusional' word makes the idea easier to digest for people who still have a foot in the cynical and negative world and are just discovering how powerful a positive attitude can be in their lives."[4]

Delusional positivity. Consider that borrowed.

Which Soundtracks Should You Borrow?

All of them.

At the beginning of this journey, don't waste time judging which ones are worthy of your new playlist. Just write down any soundtrack that's even mildly interesting to you. If that seems like a lot of work, take out your phone and tell me how many photos you currently have on it. I've got 19,928 on mine. Don't pretend you're not good at collecting stuff.

Speaking of phones, if you don't have a notebook handy because you're not a dorky writer who has a billion notebooks, snap a photo of a soundtrack instead. Start an album and throw a new one in it every time you see something that makes you curious. They don't all have to be amazing either.

My soundtracks range from "Small spark" to "That's what's up!" The phrase "delusional positivity" is on the small-spark end of the spectrum. It's a soundtrack I added to my playlist, but I probably won't think about it too often. On the other end of the spectrum are the soundtracks I can't stop talking about. Those are the ones that make me shout, "That's what's up!" the first time I hear them.

That's exactly what I said to Patsy Clairmont at lunch one afternoon. She's written over thirty books and is one of the most accomplished public speakers in the country. She's in her seventies now but told me that when she wrote her first book, the edits crushed her. "The editor sent back pages covered with red ink, and it looked like the manuscript was bleeding. I asked her to use a different color next time because it was so discouraging. The second round of edits came back with green ink and now it felt like I was growing."

That's what's up!

Imagine if the next time you make a mistake or get feedback from a coworker you think of the green ink. Instead of feeling like you failed, you remember that you're growing. That's what's up! I borrowed that one the second Patsy said it, and you should too.

Borrow These First

Want a head start on your new collection of soundtracks? Here are five I've personally found helpful. Remix them according to what works for your own life. That's what usually happens. You end up tweaking them, editing them, and combining them to create something that makes sense to your unique opportunities, strengths, and challenges.

1. People are trying to give me money.

This is the soundtrack I use when going into new business conversations or opportunities. It's not magic.

I rarely walk out of those meetings with pockets full of bread, but readjusting my thinking ahead of time changes my demeanor in the meeting. I don't get stuck on all the work I have to do or the fear that I could fail the project. I remember these people are trying to give me money.

2. I'll feel awesome after.

This is the soundtrack I turn on when it's fifteen degrees outside and I don't feel like running. Instead of thinking about how cold I'm going to be, I think, "I'll feel awesome after. The after is going to be amazing. I'll feel so proud of myself. I'll get all those endorphins and lift my head high that I actually did it." I used this soundtrack to run one thousand miles in 2019. The same goes for finishing a difficult project. I know that when I finish filming a series of videos that takes months to complete, I'll feel awesome. I focus on that positive future when my present feels challenging.

3. Spare change adds up.

If my goal is to write 1,000 words, I write 1,050. If my goal is to run 3.1 miles, I run 3.3. If my goal is to email ten clients, I email twelve. I think of that extra effort like spare change. It doesn't seem like much, but it adds up. Over a year, those extra fifty words turn into five thousand. Over a year, those extra .2 miles turn into fifty. Over a year, those extra two emails turn into two hundred. I don't force myself to run ten miles if my initial goal is three, because that's the broken soundtrack of "more" at play. But a little bit of spare change is always fun to stack up.

4. Pick ROI, not EGO.

One afternoon, after reading an early draft of this book, Jenny walked in and said, "Do you want feedback or compliments?" I started laughing because that's such a perfect soundtrack question. I might want compliments in the beginning stages of the project, but the further I go in the work, the more I need actual feedback.

I remixed her question to a new soundtrack I could use in other parts of my business, not just my writing: "Pick ROI, not EGO." Instead of picking the thing that feels best for my EGO, I want to pick the thing that has the best ROI: return on investment. This one should be plastered in every conference room in corporate America. When I shared it with colleagues, they shook their heads and proceeded to tell me stories of leaders who threw every bit of data out the window as they led in a different direction with their EGOs.

5. Pivot, don't panic.

When the coronavirus turned my world upside down in the spring of 2020, I had a simple choice to make: panic or pivot. Earlier in my life, I would've obsessed about the news, binged on social media doomsayers, and stayed stuck for weeks, if not months. I would've eaten macaroni and cheese at all hours of the day and put on twenty pounds of these-sweatpants-are-so-forgiving weight. I did that when I lost my job in 2001 during the dot-com bubble. But this time I'd just spent two years researching the power of soundtracks and knew what I needed to do.

I wrote "Pivot, don't panic" on a notecard. I repeated that soundtrack to myself and anyone else who would listen. I started a new YouTube channel. I invested in teaching virtual events when live events got canceled. I wrote a new keynote called "Pivot, Don't Panic" and began teaching it to clients around the world. I pivoted a thousand different ways, and I'll do it all over again the next time life throws me a curveball.

> "Do you want feedback or compliments?" If you want to get better, you know which one to pick.

The World Is Your Oyster—or in This Case, Your Record Shop

There's no limit to the number of soundtracks you can borrow. There's no minimum either. You're in control of the whole process. Go at your own pace and collect them in whatever way makes the most sense for you. It's impossible to fail this activity.

It can also be a lot of fun, but the real fun begins when you start creating your own. If you wrote down a few while reading this chapter, you already have the beginning of a great playlist.

If not, don't worry. I'll show you how to make some of the best soundtracks you'll ever hear with one new question: Where do you want to win?

5. Win the Week

Despite believing the soundtrack "I think I can be a public speaker and an author" in 2008, I hit a bit of a snag in 2017.

That was the year my book *Finish* came out and the year I got stuck. I didn't decide to stop writing. There was no official proclamation or retirement tour. I just looked up one day and realized I hadn't written for a year and there was no new book on the horizon.

That's not a big deal if you have a full-time job and write books on the side. But that's not the case with me. I only do two things: I write books and then I give speeches about those books. If I wasn't writing, then eventually public speaking would dry up too and I'd probably have to become a coal miner. I don't know much about coal except that it's dirty, but I live near Kentucky so I could probably figure it out.

The less I wrote, the louder my overthinking got. In hindsight, that makes sense. If action eliminates overthinking, then inaction breeds it. Since I wasn't physically engaged in the action of writing, I started overthinking more. I got caught in a nasty cycle.

Overthinking makes you feel stuck, which means you don't act. When you're not busy acting, you have more time and energy to overthink. All that additional overthinking makes you feel even more stuck, which leads to more inaction. Guess what that inaction turns into? Overthinking. Guess what that overthinking turns into? Inaction. I repeated that little loop thousands of times.

If I got near a laptop or thought about jotting down an idea, I'd hear soundtracks about how difficult writing the next book was going to be.

"You don't even have a good idea yet. Until you have a perfect idea you can't start writing."

"You've written six books—you don't have anything left to say."

"The stakes are higher than they've ever been before."

"All your peers are getting so far ahead of you."

After about eighteen months of starting and stopping, quitting and cursing, I'd had enough. I wanted to win again. I was tired of being stuck and knew I'd need a few soundtracks to spur me on. I played around with several but ultimately settled on the most obvious one I could come up with: "Writers write." That's it. If I was going to be a writer, I had to write.

Saying it's one thing, doing it's another. I had a win in sight: I wanted to write a book. I had a soundtrack to help get me there: "Writers write." Now I needed actions. For three months, when I wasn't traveling for speaking engagements and doing other things that actually made money, I'd sneak away to a coffee shop to write my new book. Why? Because writers write.

I was usually waiting at the front door for the employees to open it in the morning and would stay there until I lost most of the feeling in my legs. I'd tell you which coffee shop, because it's delightful, but I don't want you to take my seat. One hundred words became one thousand words became ten thousand words. Eventually, I had a fifty-thousand-word book that no one will ever read.

At least I hope not, because it's terrible.

I assure you that it's not just two hundred pages of "All work and no play makes Jack a dull boy," but it's not good. It's a collection of one hundred short, funny essays that made me laugh out loud in the coffee shop but would probably bore other people to tears. I wrote 345 words about why black coffee is the CrossFit of hot beverages because it's impossible for you to drink it without letting me know you drink it, and 400 words about how I kind of hope the dirt bike guy in our neighborhood crashes. Not enough to hurt him—though he'd definitely get scraped up since he hasn't worn a shirt since 2003—but just enough to ensure

> **The overthinking loop: Overthinking leads to a lack of action. A lack of action leads to more overthinking.**

that his dirt bike is never able to do midnight wheelies again in front of our house. Publishers will not be lining up for this one.

That's okay though, because the goal of writing that wasn't to release a book. It was to release me. I was creatively stuck, so I created a new soundtrack—writers write—and then turned it into action. That was a good start, but I still needed to write a new book I could actually sell. That was a much bigger win and would require more than just one new soundtrack. So I turned to Mr. Rogers.

Mr. Rogers Was Onto Something

Writing my first six books was a torturous process for me, in part because that's the soundtrack we writers have collectively bought into. One famous quote that's attributed to dozens of different people says, "Writing is easy. You just open a vein and bleed." Oh, the melodrama. A friend who was finishing a book once told me, "When you write, you always hate your book and you hate yourself."

I decided I needed to retire those negative soundtracks and create a new one to write my book. I had this crazy idea that writing didn't have to suck. I wanted something simple that could set the tone for the book you're reading right now. I needed a soundtrack for a book about soundtracks. I kicked around a lot of different words from my collection of ideas—shout-out Dorothy Parker—but ultimately settled on "light and easy."

Imagine if the hardest thing you have to do at your job was light and easy. Instead of dreading the year-end report you prepare for the leadership team, what if it felt light and easy? What if the budget you had to present at the sales conference was light and easy? What if standing on the scale was light and easy? What if the parent-teacher meeting for your high schooler was light and easy? Take anything challenging in your life and think what would happen if you retired the frustration you have about it and instead replaced it with a soundtrack that said "light and easy."

I scribbled those three words on a Post-it note and stuck it on the window I look out every day at my desk. From here on out, the writing process was going to be light and easy. That was the new soundtrack I was going to listen to. No more saying things like, "I'm going to the coal mine to write my book." (Coal miners should regularly punch writers in the face, by the way, for how often we compare the difficulty of selecting a superb adjective to the difficulty of commuting to the earth's core for work.) No more heavy feet as I walked to my desk, as if I was being led to the gallows. No more saying, "I hate this process."

This book and every book to come was going to be written with a brand-new soundtrack: light and easy. It wasn't easy to believe at first. I had a lot more broken soundtracks than I imagined. Every time I'd hit a speed bump with an idea, they would get mouthy: "See, writing is so hard. Check out Instagram instead." "Writing comes so easy to everyone else." "Non-fiction books are the worst. Write detective novels instead."

My overthinking kept getting louder, so I kept creating new soundtracks.

I wrote down, "I love writing this book!" and hung that on my wall. It helped me get through those first frustrating thirty minutes whenever I sat down to write. I love it once I'm in the middle of it, but I forget that at the beginning.

I wrote down, "Three pages is plenty" to combat the broken soundtrack that told me, "Every time you sit down to write you should be able to finish the whole book." Talk about an unkind soundtrack. I felt like a failure every time I wrote because I didn't complete the whole book in one sitting. "Three pages is plenty" was a much kinder path, and I usually ended up with four pages anyway because of my "spare change adds up" soundtrack.

For months and months, I just kept creating new soundtracks and then turning them into new actions so that I could complete the book.

It was working well, and I decided to build on my momentum with something I call *overwhelming action*. If I've got a big goal, like writing a book, running a half marathon, or not eating queso every night as if it's some sort of melty vegetable, I try to overwhelm the goal with action to make sure I accomplish it. I wasn't going to just hope writing the book felt light and easy; I was going to get creative and deliberate. Enter Nike.

Want to accomplish a difficult goal? Throw overwhelming action at it.

Their designers spent years trying to help runners break the two-hour marathon record. It was one of the last big records in competitive running. In order to give their athletes the greatest shot at the record, they created a new shoe called the Nike Vaporfly 4% Flyknit. (The 4% in the name comes from the promise that they will help you run 4 percent faster.) Created with a full-length carbon fiber plate, the shoes are angled in a way that propels you forward.

They're incredibly light, deeply cushioned, and undeniably weird. They look like what an elf would wear if that elf was also in the movie *Tron*. The back of the shoe even comes to a sharp angle that is perfect for working in the Keebler tree making delicious E.L. Fudge cookies.

I saw them one day while buying a different pair of shoes. I picked them up and they were the lightest shoe I'd ever held. I tried them on and they felt easy to run in.

I'm wearing them right now as I write this.

I bought them because sometimes a new soundtrack needs a little help to be firmly replaced. They sit in their box beside my desk, and the only time I wear them is when I write this book. Like a neon-green Mr. Rogers, when I come in to work on the book, I take off my other shoes and put on my light and easy writing shoes.

I told the woman at the shoe store, a serious runner who I knew from around town, what I was doing when I bought them. She looked at me like I was a lunatic. *Better keep that idea to myself, right up until the moment I put it in the book for the whole world to see.* We don't bat an eye when an athlete like LeBron James spends hours on his pregame ritual, but I wear one pair of nuclear-green carbon fiber shoes in my office and everyone loses their mind.

For a solid year, the shoes were never worn outside. I only put them on for two- or three-hour writing sessions. I didn't bring them to the coffee shop when I'd work on the book, because that's how you get a nickname in a small town, but it worked. Call it priming, call it the placebo effect, call it silly. I don't care, because it worked. Like slipping into an old pair of pajama pants that tell you the day is done, when I put these on I knew it was go time. They were a bright green, bouncy, physical trigger that it was time to put in some work and the whole process was going to be light and easy.

As a reward for finishing the book, I'll get to run a half marathon in them. A friend pointed out that running a half marathon is a terrible reward and more like a form of punishment, but what does he know?

You might never run a race or write a book, but if you want a simple way to see what new soundtracks would help your life, take out your calendar and ask yourself, "Where do I want to win this week?" You've got something that matters headed your way, and the more new soundtracks you use, the easier it will be to accomplish it.

Karen Is the Worst

Group projects in high school are a great way to learn that the world is full of lazy people. I tell my kids this all the time because they hate group projects and I'm not great at parenting advice. Sometimes they tell me, "I can't wait until I'm out of high school and don't have to work with people who won't carry their own weight," at which point I have just the most delightful laugh to myself.

You're going to work with difficult people. You might even be able to see a few of them from where you're sitting right now. Do you have the guy who cuts his fingernails in his cubicle at your job? That guy is everywhere!

Instead of just floundering about with our calendars and trying to figure out where we want to win, let's get specific. Let's start with the thing this planet is crawling with: people.

Looking at the week ahead, where do you want to win with the people in your life?

The reason you should ask that question is that you have a soundtrack for everyone in your life. You know that's true. Right now there are certain people who can cause a cacophony of soundtracks to play just by sending you a text message. You don't even have to read the text and you're already fired up with a heated response. Let's pretend that person's name is Karen, because it probably is.

You look on your calendar and realize you have an important meeting with her on Thursday. You need her approval on a project, and you know if you roll into that situation with broken soundtracks blaring, the whole thing will be a mess. What's the win? A good meeting. Quick approval. Less stress. It could be anything. Now, what are the soundtracks you're hearing?

Maybe the first thing you write down is "Karen is the worst." That's a good thought—I'm glad you noticed that you tend to overreact to anything she does. But "Karen is the worst" isn't a soundtrack; it's a statement. We can't really do anything with that. Replacing your soundtracks is about identifying what soundtracks you've been listening to and then owning the responsibility of changing them.

If we had coffee and you told me, "Karen is the worst," I'd tell you to pull the thread. What's behind that? What does that mean? It might hit you immediately or it might take a few minutes, but eventually you'd probably say something like, "She only reaches out when she needs something" or "She's unqualified for her job" or "She got the promotion I wanted."

Replacing your soundtracks is about identifying what **soundtracks** you've been listening to and then owning the **responsibility** of **changing** them.

We've only gone one layer deep and we've already got better soundtracks we can work on.

"She only reaches out when she needs something." What's behind that? Maybe the real soundtrack is that you feel terrible when people ask you for things you can't fulfill. You hate to tell people no, and you believe the broken soundtrack that says having a boundary is selfish. What if you could retire that? The reality is that there will always be Karens at every company, but if you retire the broken soundtrack "I'm not allowed to say no," you'll feel a lot better.

Write down that new soundtrack: "I get to have boundaries."

What about the next one? "She's unqualified for her job." Maybe she is—she is the worst, after all. But pull the thread. A few layers deep you could have a soundtrack that says, "She's progressed further than I have with fewer qualifications because she's braver. She's done far more with her career with far less because she's so confident. If I weren't afraid, I could too."

What? This Karen is turning into a gold mine of self-awareness for you! With just a few tugs on the thread, we've gone from "Karen doesn't have the right degree" to "I wish I was bold enough to ask for the opportunities she asks for."

Maybe you write down, "I want to be more confident in the meeting," or an even bigger life soundtrack, "It's time to be brave."

Moving on to the third soundtrack: "She got the promotion I wanted." Again, maybe she did, but what's behind that? I'm always surprised when I ask people questions like that, because their broken soundtracks are often telling them, "There won't be another promotion like that. That was the last one. I'm stuck and this is the job I'll always have." You'd think the gap between "Karen got a promotion" and "No company in the entire world will ever give me a promotion" would be impossible to leap, but broken soundtracks don't play fair. They're a form of fear, and fear is always distorted.

When I bumped into my own Karen situation and saw a conference call I wanted to go well coming up on my schedule, I asked the question, "What's true?"

What's true is that my difficult coworker just wanted to get the project finished, not complicate my life. What's true is that we both wanted the same thing: to make our boss happy. What's true is that we were all stressed out at the deadline we'd been given.

When I brought those true soundtracks to the meeting, the whole thing went a lot better and I felt like I won. Thanks, Karen.

You're Somebody's LEGO

You've got a soundtrack for every person in your life, but you also have one for everything you have to do. Your responsibilities as a parent, spouse, and employee are crawling with soundtracks. Take your calendar back out and look at your to-do list. Where do you want to win?

Where in your life do you want to succeed? Where could you be making faster, easier, better decisions? What do you want to improve? What do you want to dominate? What do you want to crush?

When I asked myself that question, the answer was obvious: sales.

I worked in corporate marketing for fifteen years. The sales department was a completely different organization that I knew very little about. Then, when I started my own business eight years ago, I learned something quickly: I was now in sales. I had to sell myself, my services, and my books. I wanted to be awesome at that and knew I'd need to replace a few soundtracks to get there.

I decided to jump right into my broken soundtracks related to selling. One was, "If I keep pushing my business so often, people will be angry at me." This one happens because if you're new to sales, you might unknowingly think about the worst version of it. It's easier to remember a negative example than a positive one, and you might associate sales with a sleazy salesman from a movie or a bad customer experience you had. When that happens, you mentally transform from an entrepreneur passionately sharing something you care about in a way that will serve people into a vacuum cleaner salesperson trying to trick widows into buying complicated vacuums they can't afford.

But is that true? Do people get mad if you share your business with them? I'm never mad when someone sells me something amazing that I need. I love going to REI. I love outdoor gear, even if there's a zero percent chance I will ever do the activity. That's the magic of that store—it makes me feel like I could get into deep underwater spelunking if I just owned the right headlamp system. I did briefly—or rather my wife did, because I gave it to her for Christmas. She returned it promptly. It had a belt pack battery the size of a VCR. I'm good at gifts.

I've never walked out of REI and thought, "I'm so mad that they sell ski coats! Stupid REI always telling me about the wonderful ski coats they have!" Instead, I walk out trying to figure out new reasons I need to buy the new things they sell.

One Christmas, LEGO sent us six catalogs in the mail. They weren't really different. They just moved around the same one hundred products they were pushing that year. It was like the catalog version of Taco Bell ingredients. I didn't care at all. I was excited to see each one. Why? Because I love LEGO.

I wanted to win at sales, so I decided I needed a new soundtrack. After a little bit of brainstorming, I wrote down, "I'm somebody's LEGO."

Did it work? Well, I sold you this book, soooooo . . .

What about you? What do you want to win this week?

The answers can be anything:

- I want to be more confident in my sales meeting.
- I want to make twenty cold calls even though I feel like making zero.
- I want to run ten miles despite the fact that it's 22 degrees outside.
- I want to have more fun at that dinner party.

Once you've got a win, ask yourself, "What soundtrack will encourage me to accomplish my goal this week?" You could say:

- I am as knowledgeable as anyone about this product.
- I'm not *selling* to twenty people today; I'm *serving* twenty people.

- I'll feel awesome after my run.
- I've never regretted time spent with friends after I've done it.

Now that you've got a win and a soundtrack to propel you, ask, "What actions will I need to take?"

- I will research one thing to say related to our product launch for the sales meeting.
- I will make ten calls before lunch and ten calls after lunch, because doing them all at once is too intimidating.
- I will give myself permission to run on the treadmill at the gym because that counts.
- I will ask my spouse who else is going to the party so that I can look forward to seeing a few friends.

If you do a few rounds of this exercise and actually do the actions, you'll create something really helpful: momentum. That's what happened to me in 2008. I found a small, obvious win after reading that email from the event planner who asked me to speak at the conference. I wanted to crush the first paid speaking gig I'd ever been offered.

Then I started listening to a new soundtrack: "I think I can be a public speaker." Finally, I added about a billion actions to make sure I accomplished the win and proved the soundtrack true. I spent weeks writing the first speech. I reviewed all the content with a consultant I knew. I gave the speech to my friend Jeff in my living room. I don't mean I handed him a copy to read. I mean I performed it live. The. Whole. Thing. Think Jeff on a couch, me striding confidently between our gas fireplace and 22-inch Michael Scott plasma TV, pretending that there were a thousand people in the room. Yes, I'm a better speaker now than I was then, but overall the speech went well enough to feel like a win.

Ask yourself:

1. **Where do I want to win this week?**
2. **What soundtracks will help?**
3. **What actions can I take?**

That win only strengthened my belief in the soundtrack and my willingness to invest in even more actions for the next speech.

Flip Your Way to a Win

A win is a great way to surface a new soundtrack, but what if you can't find one?

What if you bust out that calendar, stare at it for a few minutes, and start overthinking everything you have to do? Suddenly, what was supposed to be a helpful exercise to create new soundtracks turns into a breeding ground for broken ones. Fear not. That's actually a perfect place to be. We can work with that as long as we do one thing.

Instead of fighting your broken soundtrack, flip it.

6. Don't Fight It, Flip It

I once had a boss who wouldn't let me use the bathroom during work hours.

He had a timer on his desk that he used to track every minute of productivity during the day. If I needed to go, he would hit pause, making sure that the ninety seconds in the bathroom didn't count toward the hours I owed him.

The official company policy was "flex time," which is supposed to mean you work the hours that best fit your life but actually meant, "We flex all over your nights and weekends." It's hard being managed by a workaholic, because you constantly feel lazy. He'd send emails at night, text messages on the weekend, and loved launching big projects at Christmas.

He even kept a checklist to make sure you maximized your commute. There was an approved list of educational podcasts he expected you to listen to if you had to drive anywhere. It was like the state-run media in North Korea only stricter.

One year we raised the company's revenue by 48×. Let me repeat that, because it sounds made up: we increased the revenue by a factor of 48×. Know what he said when he found out? "Should have been 50×." We didn't have a party to celebrate. No one cheered in the office. I asked if we could get a cake for the breakroom and he said, "Do you think Elon Musk is eating cake right now?" How do you even answer a riddle like that? I trudged back to my desk and moved on to the next project.

The worst part is, I couldn't quit. He was the only person in our small town who would hire me. I was trapped. I spent seven long years walking into the same office, waiting for him to start that timer all over again, knowing that whatever I accomplished that day wouldn't be good enough.

Finally, it came to a breaking point. It was a cold February afternoon and I had just landed back in Nashville after a visit to Houston. The trip was stressful. In addition to the pressure of speaking at a big event, the car service broke down on the side of the interstate on the way back to the airport. I'd made the most of it, working next to an underpass and the hum of vehicles whipping by at seventy miles an hour, because I didn't want to seem like I was wasting company time. Even in the breakdown lane I was on the clock! Then I worked on the flight home and listened to a podcast in my car as I headed back to my house. The day was technically over, but I knew I should go back to work to finish up a few last things. As I pulled into the office, I said something I'd said a thousand times before: "This guy sucks. I have to quit."

There was only one problem, one small wrinkle in my escape plan.

The bad boss in this story was me.

Something's Got to Flip

If you listen to true, helpful, and kind soundtracks, working for yourself can be a wonderful experience. This is what I've been told anyway by CEOs who seem genuinely happy, but that wasn't my experience for my first seven years as an employee of Acuff Ideas, LLC.

I was the one with the stopwatch on my desk to monitor bathroom breaks. I was the one who tried to listen to twenty-five educational podcasts a month. I was the one who would dock myself ninety seconds if I went to the kitchen to grab a coffee just to make sure I wasn't stealing time from—who? Me? The company? None of it made any sense, but there really wasn't much of a mystery. I was a terrible boss because I was listening to terrible soundtracks.

I kept hearing things like, "You've got to get ahead. Other people are doing so much better than you. If you take a ten-minute break, you'll lose all your momentum. You should be doing so much more. This whole thing could fall apart at any second."

This situation wasn't new to me. I'd wrestled with this bad-boss idea for years. My wife pointed that out when I first started the company, but it felt too tangled and difficult to really do anything about. It wasn't until I first started exploring my overthinking that things began to change. It wasn't overnight or instant. How could it be? You can quit any terrible job and leave a bad boss in the dust unless you work at home and the boss is you.

How would I storm out after turning in my notice to me? How would I flip myself off? How would I peel away in my car in a blaze of glory in my own driveway?

The process of becoming a better boss wasn't that dramatic. I just started looking at my soundtracks related to work. There were a dozen different ones playing, but they were all saying roughly the same thing: "The only way to be successful is to be hard on yourself, and if that means you're a bad boss, so be it."

I'd given that approach to running my business the old college try for seven straight years, and that felt like enough. When I retire old soundtracks, I often say out loud, "That's enough of doing it that way. Let's try something different and see what happens."

I'd spent fifteen years working in corporations before I started my own business. I had good bosses and bad bosses. This is going to surprise you, but I preferred to work for the good ones. I had more fun, got more done, and actually looked forward to work when I had a good boss. Crazy, right?

That afternoon in the driveway, I asked myself a simple question: "What would the best boss do right now?" The answer was not difficult to find. In that exact situation, the best boss would say, "You've been out of town for a few days. It's five o'clock. Go home to your family! You already worked a really full day."

That was easy to figure out because I just imagined the opposite of what the worst boss would do. And you can do the same thing right now. If you want to create a new soundtrack, pick a broken one that's loud and flip it upside down. You've identified a few in this book. Look at those and imagine what listening to the opposite of all those soundtracks might feel like. You don't have to brainstorm or dream. Just imagine a coin. One side of it is full of thoughts that aren't true, helpful, or kind. If you flipped it over, what would the other side say?

The louder the broken soundtrack is, the more obvious its opposite will be. In chapter 5, I told you one of mine was, "Every time you sit down to write you should be able to finish the whole book."

What's the flip side of finishing a whole book? Writing a few pages. That's the opposite. That's what's on the other side of the coin, which is why I came up with, "Three pages is plenty." I

If you want to create a new soundtrack, pick a broken one that's loud and flip it upside down.

didn't do a deep-dive analysis of why I thought I needed to write the whole book. I didn't sit with the broken soundtrack for hours trying to untangle it. I flipped a coin in my head, and so can you.

Deb and Bryan Meyer, a married couple from Missouri, changed their relationship with money by flipping one word. "We renamed the 'emergency fund' to 'opportunity fund' and began thinking about that cash savings in a different context." It was no longer a failure bucket, full of sad dollars tucked away for a terrifying season of ramen. They replaced the soundtrack associated with that money and in doing so, transformed their entire experience.

John O'Hearn, a marketing executive in Charleston, South Carolina, changed his fear of the unknown concerning new product launches by flipping a soundtrack. "Projecting negativity around those things was super counterproductive," he said. By looking at his key objectives for his job, he'd identified a soundtrack that wasn't true, kind, or helpful. So he flipped it. He told me, "Instead of thinking, 'What if I fail?' I had to replace it with thoughts like, 'What if it's a resounding success?'"

Melissa Byers, a writer from Myrtle Beach, South Carolina, changed her approach to exercise by flipping a few soundtracks. "I had to stop telling myself the lie that unless I had all of the right clothes and gear on, the exercise didn't count." She had to retire that soundtrack and replace it with a new one: "Be active." Once she did that, she came to love her morning walks to work. "I work at home, so this consists of a walk around the neighborhood in my flip-flops while talking to my mom on the phone." That was exercise too. "I had to get my brain out of the way to see it like that." She flipped "There's only one specific type of exercise that counts" to "Lots of things count"—including phone-call walks.

I wish this process was more complicated, because then I could write a longer book and be considered the serious kind of author who poses with a pipe on the cover, but it's really not. Take out a broken soundtrack. Ask, "What's the opposite of this?" And then write down the answer.

How to Beat a Common Fear with a Simple Flip

Flipping works for minor soundtracks like turning "emergency fund" into "opportunity fund," but it also works for big, loud, scary soundtracks. Like change.

Change is the only thing every company I know has in common. At Comedy Central, we discussed how teens with

YouTube channels are competing with television shows for attention. At FedEx, we talked about Amazon developing their own shipping methods. At Nissan we talked about millennials changing their driving habits.

Change is afoot, but it's scary because of all the broken soundtracks it triggers in corporate America. One popular soundtrack says, "We have to change everything immediately." Another says, "Nothing we've done in the past will help us in the future" and "None of your current skills will translate at all to the new way of doing things." Some people also hear, "If we try this new thing once, we have to do it forever. This is the new normal."

Broken soundtracks like to traffic in absolutes. *Everything, nothing, none,* and *forever* are sure signs that you're overthinking.

Is it any wonder people are resistant to change? They've been listening to soundtracks on repeat that tell them they have to immediately change everything forever and nothing they know is going to help. I'm surprised there aren't more riots in change-management seminars.

Another indicator that you've got a broken soundtrack related to the topic of change is knee-jerk criticism. If your very first reaction to a change or a new way of working is to critique or attack it, be careful. If you can't even listen to the whole idea without knocking it, dissecting it, or pointing out flaws, there are some soundtracks at work. But that's great because once you've identified them, you can flip them.

What's the opposite of criticism? Curiosity.

What's the opposite of a dismissive statement like "That will never work here"? A curious question like "I wonder how

Broken soundtracks like to traffic in absolutes.

EVERYTHING,
NOTHING,
NONE,

and

FOREVER

are sure signs
that you're
overthinking.

that could work here?" The words aren't all that different, but the results are.

Who do you think people like to work with? Who do you think gets added to new projects? Who do you think gets invited to meetings where the future of the company is discussed? Who do you think gets promoted?

The coworker who asks thoughtful questions or the coworker who shoots down new ideas before they've even seen the light of day? There's plenty of time later to critique and iterate. There will be plenty of situations where you and the team will benefit from valuable critical thought, but that's not what we're talking about.

We're focused on your first reaction to a new idea.

What would happen if you replaced the soundtrack "Change is scary" with "Curiosity beats criticism"?

What if you wrote that down and looked at it every time you got invited to a meeting where new ideas were discussed? I think you'd probably do a much better job handling change than I did with Jeremy Cowart.

The Hotel I Couldn't See

Jeremy Cowart is a world-renowned photographer. That's not hyperbole. *The Huffington Post*, *Forbes*, and Yahoo named him the most influential photographer on the internet. From taking celebrity portraits of Taylor Swift, to capturing moments of reconciliation between warring tribes in Rwanda, to presenting at the United Nations, he's done it all. One night, on a flight to Portland, Oregon, where we would both be sharing the stage at the World Domination Summit, he told me his next big idea.

For years, he'd been secretly working on a dream about a new hotel. He envisioned a space called The Purpose Hotel, where every inch of it would be designed to help people in need. There'd be a charity water well in the lobby, each room would sponsor a hungry child, and even the soaps in the bathroom would tie back to sustainability. He excitedly told me about it for a few minutes and then did that pause people do when they're waiting for your reaction.

My face said, "That's the dumbest thing I've ever heard," and my words said, "I don't know . . . you think?" He was crushed, and years later he told me, "I thought you'd be interested or supportive of the idea. I was really disappointed by that conversation." The weird thing is, that idea wasn't even about me. I wasn't criticizing that change because I was afraid of the work it would require from me. I just found it a lot easier to criticize than to dream. I wrote a book with the subtitle *Closing the Gap between Your Day Job and Your Dream Job*, but somewhere along the way I'd picked up a broken soundtrack that said, "Dreams are dangerous. Don't get your hopes up too high."

You know who didn't react that way to Jeremy?

Horst Schulze, the cofounder of the Ritz Carlton. He's helping Jeremy develop the project. After Jeremy told me how badly I discouraged him, I decided I was done with that broken soundtrack and needed to replace it with a few new ones. When it comes to persistent soundtracks, I think it's good to replace them with more than one. At this point, I had

"Curiosity beats criticism," but maybe there was a second one I could add to the mix.

What was I really doing when someone told me their new idea and I immediately told them it wouldn't work? I was predicting the future. This felt connected to the soundtrack that you should prepare for the worst and be surprised when it didn't happen. What a bleak way to go through life that is, always expecting things to fail and then being mildly surprised when they don't.

I wrote down a new soundtrack in my notebook: "My predictions are positive."

If I'm going to predict the future, I might as well pick a positive one. The truth is, my track record for most of the terrible things I predicted would happen but didn't was roughly 0 for 345,000 anyway. And predicting a negative future for myself and other people didn't feel very good. I never walked away from that conversation and thought, "I hope I've properly discouraged that person." It felt gross, and it wasn't even accurate.

On the flip side, I always feel better when I encourage someone. I always feel good when I've made someone else feel good. And maybe their idea was going to work. Maybe Jeremy Cowart would build a hotel. I couldn't know for certain, but he wasn't asking me for anything other than encouragement in that moment.

I have a choice. I can tell you (and myself) to go for it, or I can tell you it will never work. There's plenty of time for preparation and realism later, but maybe in those initial conversations what you need isn't a wet blanket. Gordon Mackenzie, an artist at Hallmark who carved out a thirty-year career as a creative guru, explained his approach to this soundtrack in his book *Orbiting the Giant Hairball: A Corporate Fool's Guide to Surviving with Grace.*

In his final three years at Hallmark, his official title was Creative Paradox. He didn't have any real political power, but the people who came to him with new ideas didn't really know that. When they were stuck and needed some feedback, they would come sit in his office. His policy was to say that their idea was good. In one of the many speeches he gave about this practice, an audience member tried to poke a hole in Mackenzie's plan by asking, "Why tell someone an idea is good even if it isn't?" His response was perfect:

> Most companies are peppered with people who are very quick to say "no." Most newly hatched ideas are shot down before they even have time to grow feathers, let alone wings. In saying "yes" to all those who brought their ideas to me, I was simply leveling the imbalance a bit. And it worked. People who have a deep passion for their ideas don't need a lot of encouragement. One "yes" in a sea of "no's" can make the difference.[1]

The flip side of criticism is curiosity. The flip side of saying no is saying yes. The flip side of declaring why it won't work is discovering why it could. And finding the flip side is an action you can do in any area of your life.

The Truth about the Flip

Tiffany Dawn wasn't excited to see math again at her new job in Altoona, Pennsylvania. They had a shaky relationship at best that dated back to high school. "I spent years crying through high school math like algebra and geometry." I never cried during math, but I recently picked up my seventeen-year-old daughter's graphing calculator and a cold shudder ran through my entire body.

I lost the ability to help my kids with their math homework in about the fifth grade. Every year as they progress through school, my circle of shareable wisdom gets smaller and smaller. By their senior year of college, I'll probably be down to how to make jokes if a turtle pees on you during the middle of a speech. It's niche advice, but it's critical should you ever encounter the exact situation I did one night in Atlanta.

Part of the joy of growing up is putting things you're terrible at in the rearview mirror, like math. Tiffany was eager to do that, but just because high school ended doesn't mean her soundtrack did. "After high school, I spent many years saying I sucked at math." It's frustrating to get stuck on something like that for years, but it's also a clue that can help you. If you want to find a soundtrack to flip, listen to the unkind things you repeatedly say about yourself.

Unfortunately, math is one of those subjects that's like Michael Myers in the *Halloween* movie series. It refuses to go away forever. "Seven years after high school, I got a job doing payroll for a living." For someone who sucks at math, that should have been a real problem, but that's not what Tiffany discovered. "I rocked it!" she told me. She was amazing at the type of math payroll requires. The change wasn't automatic—replacing your soundtrack never is—but Tiffany worked at it.

"It still took a few years in that job to stop saying, 'I suck at math,'" she shared. But flipping it and replacing it with a new soundtrack helped: "I'm really good at everyday math; I'm not good at algebra and geometry." The key here is that she didn't lie when she flipped her soundtrack. She didn't say, "I'm the best at algebra." That wouldn't have been true. You never beat an old lie with a new lie.

She's good at everyday math. She's not good at algebra. Tiffany Dawn told herself the truth. So did I.

I didn't tell myself I was the greatest public speaker in the world when I started my adventure in 2008. That wasn't true. Ask that first audience. I threw Skittles on them between main points because I thought "Skittle Segues" would be funny. Pretty sure that's how Winston Churchill got his start too.

Choose new thoughts that generate new actions that take you new places.

Whenever I would get discouraged, I would flip "I can't be a public speaker" to "I can be a public speaker," and then I put in the work to make that new thought true. Replacing a broken soundtrack doesn't mean faking a new one. It means choosing new thoughts that generate new actions that take you new places. Like Portugal.

Europe's Worst Blister

At this point in the book, you're probably thinking that all this soundtrack stuff is easy for me because I am a beacon of positivity. I laugh in the face of hardships. I don't call them problems, I call them opportunities! You don't get rainbows without some rain.

That's not exactly the case. Allow me to explain with a rather harrowing tale from my travels abroad.

I got a blister once on the coast of Portugal.

Normally, I would covet your thoughts and prayers, but it was two years ago and it went away in about six hours without further complications. I have resilient ankles.

It happened when I was running along the edge of the ocean through the seaside town of Cascais (Kăsh-Kīsssh). Say that word out loud—it sounds like the noise a wave makes as it rolls over a colorful bed of sea glass. Cascais . . .

Have you ever used a treadmill that had a video trail you could pretend you were running on? Instead of admitting you're in the Newark Airport Ramada you can watch a loop of someone running through Wellington, New Zealand. The trail in Portugal was exactly like that except I was actually there and not in a hotel fitness center.

The waves of the North Atlantic were lapping gently on the shore. The sun was rousing the day from its nighttime slumber with a warm kiss. Tourists were frolicking in impossibly blue pools gathered along the sand as I circled the bay on my morning run along a path Christopher Columbus probably walked as a child. I wasn't thinking about any of that when I returned to our hotel room after I was done though.

"How was your run?" Jenny asked when I walked into the room.

"I got a blister," I said.

Poof.

The entire experience, the coast of Portugal, the luxury hotel, the abundant access to at least a hundred varieties of sardines— all of it vanished in the face of my pencil-eraser-sized blister.

That is how powerful my negative thinking is.

I'm not an outside observer to broken soundtracks. I'm your mayor. *Oh, you think darkness is your ally. But you merely adopted the dark; I was born in it, molded by it. I didn't see the light until I was already a man, and by then it was nothing to me but BLINDING!*[2]

I made the entire Iberian Peninsula disappear with the arrival of a blister. When I tell you that I tend to be negative, I mean it from the bottom of my critical heart.

But something unexpected happened to me.

The more I researched what it takes to turn overthinking from a super problem into a superpower, the more I kept bumping into positive thinking. *Oh no*, I groaned to myself, *I don't know how to speak that language.*

Why can't the solution be something easier, like Mandarin? Tell me complex Chinese is the answer!

Don't make me become one of those people I mock on Instagram who are always selling video courses—and you're not going to believe this, they just extended the registration period they swore they were closing, because they didn't want you to miss it!

You can have my negativity when you pry it from my cold, dead hands.

Alas, even I, with blister vision, could deny it no longer. If we're really going to create fresh soundtracks that propel us to the lives we want, we've both got some positivity in our very near future.

7. Zig Your Way to Positive Thinking

Technically, the reason rain started getting into my Volkswagen GTI was that I pulled in front of someone and caused a minor accident. Thank goodness I wasn't on my phone at the time writing an earth-shattering tweet, or my wife, Jenny, would have murdered me. I was just really excited about pizza and cut off a college student when I was turning into the De-Sano's parking lot. That's just one more example of my enthusiasm for pizza wreaking havoc in my life.

Both doors on the driver's side needed to be replaced, so I brought it to a local autobody shop. They fixed it for a few thousand dollars and then gave me back the car. Everything was great until it started to rain in Nashville. We get more inches of rain than Seattle every year, but we don't brag about it all the time. One morning, my youngest daughter pointed out that there was a puddle at her feet in the back seat of my car.

"Did you bring a puddle with you?" I asked, hoping that was the case. "Are your feet anxious today?" I'm no doctor, but maybe that was the problem. My daughter has sweaty, nervous feet. Don't judge me as a parent. She was born that way and we love her.

I dried the floor mat with a few paper towels and crossed my fingers. That accomplished nothing, because a few days later when it rained again, the puddle came right back. Here's where my broken soundtracks stole the day. I refused to call the autobody shop to have them fix the leak. Why? Because asking people to do their jobs is a hostile confrontation, and confrontation must be avoided at all costs.

Where did that come from? A broken soundtrack. You might be familiar with it too. Sometimes it goes by the name "There's something wrong with my meal but I don't want to bother the waiter so I'll just choke this food down, it's fine."

That's not very helpful, but it's nothing compared to the other soundtrack that I uncovered in this situation. That one tells me, "Everyone is trying to rip you off." Based on how often I hear that, you'd think a big bank stole our family farm when I was a child.

Now, just the thought of calling the autobody shop blasts those two soundtracks: (1) This is a confrontation. (2) They're going to take advantage of you. In response to the negative music, I put off the call for a day or two or six weeks. Fine, I said it. I avoided calling them for six weeks, which, funny coincidence—this is going to make you laugh more than it did Jenny—is exactly the same amount of time it takes for standing water to grow mold.

I wasn't lazy during those six weeks while I avoided the call. I was busy wrestling with overthinking and trying to postpone the inevitable. I put a beach towel on the floorboard and soaked up the water. I bought a box of moisture-eating gel to ride shotgun with my now seven-pound, sopping-wet beach towel. I propped up my trunk each night and wedged the world's heaviest dehumidifier into the car like that was a normal thing completely sane people did.

Counselors often say that one of the first signs of denial is when you lift a sixty-pound dehumidifier into your car because you don't want to call an autobody shop. I might have gone on that way for the rest of my life, but it started to smell.

"What is that odor?" Jenny would ask.

"I don't smell anything," I'd lie through my overthinking teeth.

"It smells like a swamp in here," she'd say.

"Not sure what you're talking about," I'd reply, taking deep breaths through my mouth.

It was a classic battle between mold and overthinking, but eventually *Stachybotrys* won. That's black mold's scientific name. Once you've spent six weeks riding around with someone, you tend to know them pretty well.

I finally bit the bullet and called the autobody shop, expecting the worst. Know what happened instead? It was one of the easiest conversations I've ever had in my life. The owner was horrified and couldn't have been more apologetic. He fixed the car immediately and didn't make me pay another cent. The phrase "toxic mold" is probably on my CARFAX, but what it should really say under mechanical history is "overthinking."

The more I worked on this book, the more examples I found like this where broken soundtracks were stealing my time, creativity, and productivity. Or in this case, my ability to breathe. *You've gone too far this time, overthinking. I draw the line at breathing.*

Overthinking doesn't play fair, so we won't either.

Overthinking wasn't playing fair, so I decided I'd better raise my game too. I needed to dig deeper into understanding the power of soundtracks if I was really going to win. That journey took me to a place I never thought I'd go: positive affirmations.

All Roads Lead to Zig

Seth Godin is a *New York Times* bestselling author of eighteen books. He's a marketing savant who *Business Week* called one of the most influential thinkers in business, and he's the person I've most closely modeled my career after. He's also not prone to the motivational fluff that clogs up social media these days.

One morning, while listening to *The Moment* podcast, I heard Seth tell a story about how his first publishing project was rejected eight hundred times. For a solid year, every single door was slammed in his face. That's the kind of failure that would knock most people right out of an industry.

When the host, Brian Koppelman, asked Seth how he talked himself through the challenge, his answer surprised me: "It wasn't self-talk, it was Zig-talk. Zig Ziglar talked to me every day for three hours. For three hours a day, for three years, I listened to this guy. I knew it by heart because there were only 72 hours of stuff. That voice in my head took over because I didn't have the voice I needed in my head."[1]

As if that wasn't a strong enough endorsement, Seth even declared, "The only thing that kept me from quitting and getting a job as a bank teller were the tapes that Zig did."[2]

When one of your heroes mentions one of his heroes, your ears perk up. If you're not familiar with Zig Ziglar, he was one of the forefathers of motivational thought in America. His books have sold millions of copies, including his bestseller *See You at the Top*. He traveled the world sharing the power of positive thinking for more than forty years and spoke to audiences at thousands of events.

I was surprised Seth was such a big fan of Zig's work but filed that fact away somewhere in my head and moved on with my life.

Weeks later, while reading Tim Grahl's book *Running Down a Dream*, Ziglar popped back up. Grahl, a book marketing expert who once had five clients on the *New York Times* bestseller list at the same time, wrote that he did Zig's daily affirmations twice a day for thirty days.

My curiosity was piqued. I dug a little deeper into Zig's affirmations and was able to easily find them online. The plan wasn't complicated. For thirty days in a row, first thing in the morning and last thing before bed, you're supposed to read them out loud while looking at yourself in the mirror.

Oh, good grief.

The idea of standing in front of the mirror twice a day while telling myself things like "I am an honest, sincere, hardworking person. I am tough but fair and sensitive" felt crazy.

Why don't I just add "Serenity now!" from *Seinfeld* while I'm at it?

The walls of my pessimism were crumbling though, as techniques I'd mocked for years kept coming up. Maybe there was something to repeating positive soundtracks. Perhaps there was more here than soccer moms with driftwood signs that read "Live, Laugh, Love." I started to casually ask successful people I know if they believed in positive thinking. The words they used were a little different, but they were all quietly practicing self-talk.

"I have a few sentences I tell myself every morning."

"I have a mantra I repeat to myself all day."

"I give myself a pep talk each afternoon."

The evidence was mounting. Was repeating my new soundtracks the key to making them stick? I wasn't sure, but since I was fresh off of getting my butt kicked by overthinking in the mold battle, I was willing to try anything. I decided to try positive affirmations for thirty days. What's the worst that could happen?

Me and Zig and the Mirror

There are a million different affirmations online, and I knew as a writer I would probably create my own eventually, but for my first experiment, I went straight to the source. If Zig was good enough for Seth Godin and millions of other people, he was good enough for me.

I printed out Zig's affirmations and put them by the sink in our guest bathroom to read first thing in the morning and last thing before bed.

I chose that location because before I even started, Jenny said, "I don't want you doing that in the bathroom we share."

Despite the scientific evidence that priming yourself with positive soundtracks was a real thing, she didn't think she could make out with me after hearing me recite the affirmations in the mirror while she brushed her teeth. Fair enough.

The first thing I noticed while doing them was that I didn't believe about 85 percent of what I was saying to myself.

For example, one of the statements says, "I take pride in my appearance." That's not true. I don't ensconce myself in velvet (second *Seinfeld* reference in the chapter), but I don't dress up often. This affirmation was particularly hard to say out loud while looking at the same blue Snowbird ski shirt I wear at least three times a week. I'm the kind of person that if I put on a belt and a collared shirt, friends immediately say, "Whoa, what's going on today? You headed to a funeral?"

The longer I went through the list of affirmations those first few days, the more I realized most of those statements weren't currently true about myself.

That's usually what initially happens when you start repeating a new soundtrack. You feel like a liar. It's weird to say things about yourself that aren't true—yet. What's funny though is that if you're an overthinker, you've already done that exact same thing for years; you just haven't noticed because you weren't saying them out loud.

"Everyone is trying to take advantage of me" is every bit as big a lie as "I take pride in my appearance," but one has played a thousand times without me ever once calling it out because it's hidden under the cloak of an internal thought.

Reading the affirmations encouraged me to deal with an important question: Why is it so easy to repeat negative soundtracks about myself internally and so hard to repeat positive soundtracks about myself externally?

Maybe the answer goes all the way back to chapter 1. Maybe it's because the brain can be kind of a jerk. Maybe it was cognitive bias: I'd been collecting evidence of my negative soundtracks for years, so it was easy to believe those and hard to believe new ones. Maybe it was just plain old fear.

Why is it so easy to repeat negative soundtracks internally and so hard to repeat positive soundtracks externally?

I honestly didn't know, but I felt like I was being given a simple choice: Did I want these new things to be true of me, or did I want to listen to the same broken soundtracks I'd always heard? Did I want this list of words like *persistent, optimistic, loyal,* and *disciplined* to be reflective of who I am? The answer was an overwhelming "Yes!"

Nothing particularly magical happened immediately. The progress of repeating the soundtracks was more of a slow burn that I noticed in small ways. Like one afternoon when the flight attendant was passing out drinks and I took a Diet Coke from her because I thought it was mine. I didn't know the lady sitting in the window seat had ordered one too. I said, "Did you get a Diet Coke? Oh, sorry, here you go," and handed it to her.

I immediately felt the temptation to overthink that meaningless interaction and play a broken soundtrack that said, "I grabbed that because I'm inherently greedy. I have a real greed issue. I'm the greediest person ever." Then I would have listened to my brain list out examples of times I'd been greedy in the past. That's what I was expecting to happen, but instead I heard the soundtrack from Zig grow louder: "I'm a generous person. I love generosity. I just made a quick mistake. No big deal."

I was surprised how automatic it felt. I didn't need to pause and say, "Now, Jon, remember your positive soundtracks. Focus on the mirror, the mirror in your heart." It just happened automatically. It was almost as if my brain, which is already amazing at playing soundtracks, just pulled the most recent one from the shelf.

The weird thing is that "I am generous" wasn't even one of the statements I'd been reciting. It just felt like the kind of statement that would be true of the person I was becoming. I started to realize that the exact words weren't that important. The act was. The repetition was.

It didn't even have to be perfect. I missed five days out of thirty and still felt like I benefited. Even on mornings when I forgot to do it when I got out of bed, when I woke up and said the words at 9 a.m. instead of first thing, it worked. All my broken soundtracks weren't gone, but I was entering each day with some fresh ones. In stressful situations, I found myself thinking, "I am bold, authoritative, and confident, yet humble."

I also kept finding examples of why this practice was working. In *The Invisible Gorilla*, Christopher Chabris and Daniel Simons detail how radiologists often miss obvious things, like a guidewire left in a vein, when they review X-rays because of the illusion of attention. "People assume that radiologists will notice anything anomalous in an image, when in reality they, like the rest of us, tend to best see what they are looking for in an image."[3] If you tell a radiologist to look for a pulmonary embolism, it's easy for them to completely miss the guidewire, which shouldn't be there.

You can fix that problem though. "If you tell radiologists to find the guidewire in a chest X-ray, they will expect to see one and will notice it."[4] That's what my Zig experiment felt like. I was just telling myself to look for positive things, and suddenly they were a whole lot easier to find.

Going to the Source for a Deeper Look at the Affirmations

Ten years ago, I had the opportunity to have lunch with Zig, his wife, Jean, and his son, Tom. Though our time was short, Zig taught me a handful of things that I'm still applying to my life today. After I tried the affirmations, I was curious to know more about why they work. Zig passed away in 2012, but Tom was more than happy to discuss the potential of this simple exercise with me over a long phone call.[5]

Zig's affirmations were part of his Self-Talk Cards, but Tom told me he'd been using them for much longer than that on-stage with live audiences. He also employed them around the house. Tom said, "When I was sixteen, I applied for a job at the Athlete's Foot. Before I went, I told my dad why they would never hire me. I was just sixteen, I'd never had a job, etc. Dad looked at me and said, 'Wait a second. You've had sixteen years of hard work, discipline, honesty, character, and integrity.'"

Those might just sound like nouns, but they're much more than that. "Dad just went down the affirmation list. He said, 'When they ask you why you're qualified for the job, that's what you tell them.' Of course I got the job."

When his sixteen-year-old son told him about a broken soundtrack, Zig helped him create a new one. But what if he didn't get the job? What if something negative happened to Zig, the master of positive affirmation? How would he respond then?

That's the question, isn't it? Bad things happen. To me, to you, to the world in general. How can you stay so focused and repeat positive soundtracks in the face of negativity? I asked Tom that directly, and it ended up being the bulk of our conversation.

"Dad used to always say, 'It's not what happens to you that determines how far you will go in life; it's how you handle what happens to you.' He was big on the difference between reacting, which is negative, and responding, which is positive. If you go to the doctor and you get prescribed medicine, a few days later he'll call you. If you say, 'I'm broken out in hives and my tongue swelled up,' you've had a reaction to the medicine. That's negative. If you say, 'My fever's gone. My energy is back up. I feel better!' then you responded to the medicine. That's positive."

"I react to problems" versus "I respond to problems" is a subtle shift, but it's an important one. That felt like an example of flipping a soundtrack. But how do you live that out in the middle of a busy week? "You plan in advance how you're going to respond," Tom said.

"Take travel, for instance. You know if you get on a plane more than twice a year, you're guaranteed to be delayed or canceled. When that happens, you should have your plan already worked out and your attitude should already be decided. Your negative attitude isn't changing when the plane is leaving, and in a lot of cases you should be grateful they're not flying you in dangerous conditions. That's actually for your benefit."

Everything Tom said made sense, even as I continued pressing him for practical applications. That's where most positive-thinking approaches break down for me: they're good in theory but fall apart on a Tuesday. I wanted real-world solutions, not empty platitudes, so I kept playing "Stump the Ziglar" with Tom. "Okay, so you plan a better attitude for a delayed flight, but how do you really retire the soundtrack that says your day is ruined in that moment?" I asked him.

"My dad always had his most important work with him when he traveled. Every flight delay or cancelation was an opportunity to get his number one priority done." Can't you just see Zig Ziglar hunkered down in the corner of terminal B1, spending two productive hours on something he cares about when his flight back home to Dallas got delayed?

The delayed flight didn't hurt his day; it actually gave him an invitation to work on his most important projects. Zig won not just because he had a good attitude but because he tied his positive soundtracks to real actions, like bringing his work with him.

That's also such a different approach than listening to a soundtrack that blames your bad day on everyone else. Saying that the traffic ruined your day might seem minor, but what you're really saying is "I gave the traffic the power to determine the quality of my day."

Good days start with good thoughts.

We lived in Atlanta for six years, and if I let my commute tell me how my day was going to go, every day would've sucked. That's what the flashing road signs would have said: "Peachtree Center: 10 miles, 1 billion minutes. Jon's Monday: Ruined." My days were much better when I chose my thoughts before I even left the house.

Beyond the Bright Side

Flight issues are the kind of thing you can prepare for, but what about negative situations that catch you off guard? In situations like that, is it better to just be positive and push through? Should you always just look on the bright side of things?

"No," Tom said, which surprised me. "It's not negative to identify a problem. In fact, it's positive because now you're in the position to work on the solution. It's not negative to admit you have a problem. You don't have to be positive about everything. If your life is difficult right now because of things that have happened to you, it's not negative to acknowledge that. It's only negative if you stay there. What you want to focus on is the solution."

The week I interviewed Tom was also the week I realized the revenue from one part of my business was down 70 percent from the previous year. I'm not amazing at math, but that didn't feel like a positive thing. I started to overthink my relationship with the person who helped run it and got really frustrated. They were taking advantage of me, just like I thought the autobody shop was going to before I called about the leak in my car. The more I thought about it, the louder my old soundtracks got.

"This is all his fault. He hasn't been doing his job because he's trying to damage my business. I can't believe he's doing this to me!" Then a shame soundtrack jumped in, because once the door is cracked open, my soundtracks pile in like a rugby scrum. "This problem is just the tip of the iceberg. This whole division of your business is a train wreck because you don't know how to run a business. You've been asleep at the wheel and you'll never catch up now."

Round and round I went, getting angrier with each listen. Do you know what I was doing in that moment? Focusing all my time, creativity, and productivity on the problem instead of the solution. I was overfeeding the problem and starving the solution. That wasn't getting me anywhere. I decided to switch soundtracks because the conversation with Tom was so fresh in my head.

It wasn't easy. It didn't feel natural or comfortable at first, but it was definitely the best path out of that audio melee. I asked myself, "What would it look like to put my best brainpower to the fix, not the fear?" This new soundtrack became a pause moment for me in the middle of storms.

Try it. The next time you're in the middle of a stressful situation, ask yourself, "Am I focusing on the problem or the solution?" It's simple but it works.

The next time you're in the middle of a stressful situation, ask yourself, "Am I focusing on the problem or the solution?"

JON ACUFF

#soundtracks 📷

I was tracking with Tom but still needed more clarity. So I asked him, "Is this like fake it till you make it? You just over-focus on the solution?"

"No," Tom replied. "We don't teach fake it till you make it. Dad believed in 'Tell the truth in advance.' The affirmations are true. Let's say you're a hundred pounds overweight and your goal is to lose that. Some people would say a positive affirmation like, 'I'm fit and trim and living life to the fullest.' But you're not and your brain knows that. It's not true and that creates cognitive dissonance [stress that occurs when your brain tries to believe multiple things that disagree with each other at the same time]. Instead, it's better to say what my friend Steyn Rossouw says: 'I'm getting fitter and fitter every day in every way.' That's true. Those words are an aspiration of where you are going."

I kept trying to poke little holes in the idea of positive affirmations, but Tom answered all my questions with actionable advice I could really use in tangible ways. I suppose working on an idea for forty years leads to expertise.

The conversation was encouraging and gave me greater insight into why doing an affirmation exercise worked for me. I could see the difference it made, but I still had one big question.

If positive soundtracks worked for me, would they work for you too?

8. Put the New Anthem on Repeat

I own forty-eight haircuts.

That's probably forty-eight more than you own, but allow me to explain my follicle-focused abundance. The barbershop I go to sells haircuts in packages. It's like a subscription plan for your head. I usually buy six at a time and save a dollar per haircut by paying in advance.

The last time I ran out of haircuts, my hairdresser said, "You're all out and need to buy some more. Do you want to buy your regular package or go up in number?"

"How much could I save with your biggest option?" I asked.

"With that one, the price drops from $32 to $24 per cut," she said.

What a deal. "How many haircuts is that?"

"Forty-eight," she replied.

I think we can both agree that's too many haircuts. There's no one who needs to prepay for forty-eight haircuts ahead of time. I've never met someone who said, "I don't like bringing my wallet to barbershops. I'd rather pay in advance. I'm sorry, that's just how I was raised." That's pure foolishness, and I was about to buy six when she casually remarked, "Your friend Chris just bought the forty-eight package."

Oh, hold on one second. Chris did?

I knew what she was doing. That was a soft sell. She wasn't strong-arming me toward a decision. It was real casual. *No pressure, Jon, but one of your good friends, whom you respect, bought this same thing I'm selling you.* That's how the Simpsons and their town of Springfield ended up with a monorail. The salesman mentioned that Shelbyville was going to get one, and they couldn't resist. But they're just cartoon characters. I'm different. I'm an adult. I can see through a sales pitch. Only that's not what happened.

The next thing I knew, I was shouting, "Let's do it. I'd like to buy forty-eight haircuts!" I spent over $1,000 at the barbershop after about four seconds of thought. My thinking tends to have two speeds: overthink and underthink. Guess which one that was?

When I got home, Jenny didn't seem too enthusiastic about how much money I'd saved. She seemed real hung up on the $1,000 in haircuts part of the story. Then, because she's actually good at planning, she asked a question: "How often do you get your hair cut?"

"Every three weeks," I answered.

"Well, let's run the math on that decision. If you go to the barber once every three weeks and you just bought forty-eight haircuts, how long will it take you to use them all?" That felt like a question from the SAT, and by her tone I could tell she already knew the answer.

"But the cost savings," I said, trying to distract her.

"It will take you 2.7 years to use all those haircuts. We'll have a kid in college by the time you finally finish them."

"And I bet she'll be able to go somewhere real nice because I saved so much money on my haircuts," I responded, which was probably not the point she was making. The point was probably that I'm not good at long-term planning or math or haircuts apparently. But I am good at other things, like telling people about ideas that will improve their lives. That's what my entire business is built around and is the heart of every book I've written and speech I've given.

Which is why when I had success repeating positive affirmations, I decided to share what I learned. I just can't keep good ideas to myself. My high school geometry teacher once told my mom during a parent conference, "Jon answers questions before they've been asked." I don't think he meant it as a compliment, but that's how I took it!

When I'm excited about something, I don't let you past the foyer of my house before I've shared it with you. I'll pull up a funny video, show you my new favorite book, or run upstairs to bring down a LEGO set before you've even taken off your coat. It's happened so often that Jenny started calling the things I love the most "foyer ideas."

I'd borrowed Zig's affirmations (I see you, chapter 4, you rascal), but if I was going to share positive affirmations with other people, I wanted to create my own. And not just create them—I wanted to test them, teach them, and see if they'd help other people as much as they helped me.

So I asked Mike Peasley, PhD, to help me formulate a plan, because he's great at plans and buys his haircuts in single packs.

Creating the New Anthem

The first step was to create a brand-new set of affirmations. Thanks to Dorothy Parker's wild-mind/disciplined-eye approach, I had already collected dozens. I was a year into studying overthinking and had plenty of soundtracks to sort through. I covered the walls of my office with three-by-two-foot sheets of paper and started writing down ideas where I'd see them every day.

Some were aggressively optimistic: "Boring days are afraid of me!"

Some were simple: "It isn't over until I win."

Some were hokey: "Fear is just an invitation to bravery."

Some were mopey: "I'd rather whole hurt than half hope." (That's the most emo way to say "Go for it with everything you've got!" even if you don't win.)

Some were stories that I thought might have a soundtrack hidden within them. For example, one of my handwritten notes said, "Billy Joel doesn't sell the seats to the front rows of his concerts because he got tired of only being able to see bored, rich people in the crowd. He gives away the front rows to enthusiastic fans now so that he has fun watching them while he performs. Maybe there's a soundtrack here about choosing who you surround yourself with?"

After a few weeks of writing everything down, my office looked a bit like a scene from *A Beautiful Mind*. If I opened the door too quickly, those massive sheets of paper full of ideas would flap in the breeze like Celine Dion's dress in that one video where she sings about love. Satisfied that I had more than enough to work with, I started to whittle all of them down.

I wanted to create a "New Anthem," something you and I could say in the mirror for thirty days in a row. Something true, helpful, and kind. It would be a collection of positive statements that spoke to both identity and reality. An identity statement is "I've got a gift worth giving." That's about who you are. A reality statement is "Momentum is messy." That's about how life works.

The statements wouldn't be accidental but carefully chosen to address the things people tend to overthink. "Momentum is messy" addresses perfectionism. "I am the CEO of me, and I am the best boss!" focuses on taking radical responsibility for your life while at the same time being kind to yourself. With that criteria, I cut hundreds of soundtracks down to the twenty I thought worked best. I sent them to a few dozen people to see if any of them jumped out. They gave me feedback, and ten clear winners emerged.

> I am the CEO of me, and I am the best boss!

I crafted a set of instructions designed to turn the volume up even louder on the New Anthem and then tested the whole thing with more than ten thousand people.

Wait, what? Kind of breezed right by that part. That's one of the best things about my job. When I have an idea I think is exciting, it doesn't just stay in my foyer. I partner with Mike Peasley, PhD, and turn it into a research study. Then, because I've spent years nurturing an online community, I have thousands of people who will test it with me. I don't have the biggest platform in the world, but I am a Gummi Bear influencer. That's exactly what it sounds like. I talked about my love of Albanese Gummi Bears so often on Instagram that they just started sending me free bags of their product. What do you think is going to happen when they find out I mentioned them in a book? It's about to rain Gummi Bears at the Acuff house.

Delicious candy aside, Mike Peasley, PhD, and I had everything we needed. We had ten thousand participants signed up for a thirty-day challenge, a method to track progress, a private Facebook group to gather stories, and the New Anthem.

You have it too. It's right here. I'll give you the results of the study in a minute, but I couldn't wait any longer to share the New Anthem with you. We're several pages into this chapter, which is like making it all the way to my living room without hearing a foyer idea when you visit my house. It's been killing me.

I think you should do the New Anthem. I think you should start today. Once you've read through it once, I'll tell you why.

The New Anthem

For thirty days, every morning and every night, find a mirror, stand up straight, and confidently say the following out loud:

I, [your name], choose my thoughts. I know that doing my best starts with thinking my best. Like laying a path for an adventure, these thoughts will set the course for my actions.

I'm confident that what I think matters. I'm excited to see what happens next. I'm disciplined and dedicated to stick with it. Here are ten things I know:

1. Today is brand-new and tomorrow is too.
2. I've got a gift worth giving.
3. The only person standing in my way is me, and I quit doing that yesterday.
4. I am the CEO of me, and I am the best boss.
5. Winning is contagious. When I help others win, I win too.
6. Feeling uncomfortable is just a sign that my old comfort zone is having a hard time keeping up with me.
7. Momentum is messy.
8. Everything is always working out for me.
9. I am my biggest fan.
10. The best response to obstacles is to do it anyway.

In the morning

I've pulled the slingshot back. I'm not *leaving* this room, I'm *launching* from it, ready for a day of untold opportunities. I've packed honesty, generosity, laughter, and bravery for the road ahead. Watch out, world! It's time to step up, step out, and step in.

In the evening

What a day! The best part is I left myself a lot of fun things to work on tomorrow. When my head hits that pillow, I'm off the clock, storing up energy and excitement for a brand-new day.

Did You Do It?

Be honest. There's no one here but you and me. Unless you get the audio version of the book, which means it's you, me, and the most grizzled sound engineer you've ever met. I always try to make them laugh, because otherwise it's like giving a six-hour speech to an audience of one. They usually won't break character, because they're only listening for mistakes and don't even really hear what you're saying. Except for this paragraph. Now that I think about it, this one is going to be awkward to record.

Maybe you tried the New Anthem. You found a mirror, closed the bathroom door, and said it out loud to yourself. If you did, congrats. You're halfway done with today's repeat exercise. Knock it out one more time before bed tonight and you're good to go. If you didn't try it though, I don't blame you. If I were you, I might still be thinking, "What's in it for me?"

That's a good question, and it's one that every company I visit as a public speaker asks me. I can't go back to Lockheed Martin or Microsoft and say, "Remember how you liked my last speech about finishing goals? You're going to love this one. It's jam-packed with feel-good affirmations that are going to turn your frowns upside down."

Companies want you to teach them techniques that will help them make faster, better decisions. Companies want shortcuts to higher performance. Companies want more time, creativity, and productivity for the things that matter.

And you should too.

That's why I did a research study around the New Anthem eighteen months before I put it in this book. I didn't want to share anything I hadn't tested first. The goal of the study was simple. We wanted to explore three questions:

1. Does repeating positive affirmations help decrease overthinking?
2. Does decreasing overthinking help increase your productivity?
3. Does decreasing overthinking raise your success rates for goals?

To test that, we asked more than ten thousand people to repeat the New Anthem twice a day for thirty days in a row. We compared their performance before the affirmations and after the affirmations to get a read on what changed. We didn't hook up any electrodes to anyone, because those are expensive, but the study revealed more than we ever could have hoped for.

Question 1: Does repeating positive affirmations help decrease overthinking?

The first statistic we looked at was what happened to participants who repeated the New Anthem at least twenty times (morning or evening). Did their overthinking increase, decrease, or stay the same? According to the data, this group was 250 percent more likely to reduce their overthinking versus have it stay the same or increase.

If you stood in front of a mirror, despite feeling ridiculous, at least twenty times in a month and recited the New Anthem, you were 2.5 times more likely to have less overthinking than to have it stay the same or increase. A little bit of work went a long way when it came to dealing with overthinking.

I liked that data, but it wasn't strong enough proof for me. I also wanted to know if the number of times I repeated the New Anthem mattered. We studied turn-down techniques in chapter 3. Could positive affirmations be one of the best ways to lower the volume on the days our dial gets ratcheted too high? The results were positive there too. Participants who repeated twenty or more soundtracks were 46 percent more likely to decrease their overthinking than people who repeated five or fewer.

That research is a bit bonkers to me. You're 46 percent more likely to decrease your overthinking if you repeat the New Anthem twenty times versus five times. Imagine if today there was something you could do that took less than ninety seconds and made you 46 percent more likely to reduce your overthinking. There is—you saw it a few pages ago, in fact.

Question 2: Does decreasing overthinking help increase your productivity?

I had braces in seventh grade. A girl in my pre-algebra class named Patty Ericson told me that I could cut the time I had to wear my headgear in half if I also wore it at school instead of just when I was asleep at night. Fat chance, Headgear Patty. That's how a kid gets a nickname. I'll take the slow route on this orthodontic adventure, if you don't mind.

That's probably the only productivity hack I've ever rejected. We're all obsessed with them, constantly looking for ways to shave time off tasks. But what if we're overlooking the greatest waste of time in our lives—overthinking? Can you imagine how amazing it would be if all it took to raise your productivity a bit was to reduce your overthinking? Put the five-minute children's bedtime story down—which is a very real time-saving product—because I am about to blow your mind.

Participants who said the New Anthem twenty or more times versus people who said it ten or fewer times reported being more productive at working on their goal. What does that mean in a practical sense? It means they worked on their goal nine more days than people who didn't repeat the New Anthem as many times. That's a productivity gold mine, so allow me to repeat that sentence. In a thirty-day period, they worked nine more days on their goals! What if you played that out over a year? That equates to an extra 108 days of hustle for people who repeat the New Anthem. How much more would you get done if you added 108 days of effort to your goal?

Not only were the New Anthem repeaters more productive, they had 21 percent higher satisfaction with their results. At the end of the thirty days, they were happier with what they had accomplished. If you've ever thought, "How do I get more done and feel even better about my job?" please underline this whole paragraph. I think part of the reason satisfaction increased is that for that same group of people, they were 15 percent more likely to reduce their self-doubt. As self-doubt receded, satisfaction took its place.

Let's be skeptics though. Just because someone worked on a goal nine days more doesn't mean she spent all day doing it. Nobody works on a goal for eight to ten hours each day. Let's say the participants in this study only worked thirty minutes per day. In a month, nine extra days at that rate would translate into 4.5 bonus hours. In a year, that becomes fifty-four hours, or almost seven full eight-hour workdays. If your boss gave you seven extra vacation days this year, would that feel like a significant gift? It would. Do the New Anthem, reduce your overthinking, and just give that gift to yourself.

Question 3: Does decreasing overthinking raise your success rates for goals?

I shouted with joy the moment I finished my thousandth mile of the year while running one afternoon. It was December 18, the day before my forty-fourth birthday, and I remember exactly where I was. I proclaimed to myself, "That's what's up!" and picked up the pace in unbridled excitement because I couldn't believe I completed a goal that took me 352 days. I loved that moment, and I want more of them—for me and for you.

How do we get them? We find creative ways to succeed at our goals, like dealing with overthinking—which, remember, is when what you think gets in the way of what you want.

Participants who said their overthinking decreased completed 78 percent more of their goal than people who didn't decrease their overthinking. That's incredible, but also the least surprising result ever published. When you reduce the time you waste overthinking, you get more done. Imagine that. We're not done though. There's still one big number left to unwrap.

People who said their overthinking decreased were four times—that is, 400 percent—more likely to reach or almost reach their goal. Four hundred percent! Not only did they complete more than people who didn't decrease their overthinking, they were much more likely to finish the whole goal. This study just kept dunking on every expectation I had.

In summary, repeating the New Anthem helped reduce overthinking and self-doubt. It increased satisfaction and productivity. And finally, it encouraged people to work nine more days on their goals than their peers did.

> **Repeating the New Anthem helped decrease overthinking and self-doubt while increasing satisfaction and productivity.**

All of that from a simple piece of paper? Yes, and the personal stories we heard from participants added an even stronger voice to the data.

The People Speak Up

Maybe you're not a math person. I get it. I bought nearly three years of haircuts. Numbers are confusing. Give me stories, you say! Real life. The very fabric of what we are made of.

No problem. In addition to statistical data, we gathered anecdotal evidence in a private Facebook group during the month. It was an opportunity for people to interact and share their personal experiences. More than 3,500 people joined and posted thousands of points of feedback.

As I combed through all the comments, a pattern began to emerge. When you first try the New Anthem, you're going to feel foolish. Unless you've done something like this before, you are 100 percent going to feel silly standing in front of the mirror and giving yourself a pep talk. Brittni Dappen, a home-schooling mom from Washington State, said, "I feel stupid when I say the anthem. I can't say it out loud within earshot of my husband yet." It's not her husband's issue. "He would totally support me; he's my biggest cheerleader," Brittni says, but she still feels weird.

The first few times I did it, I remember declaring to my family that I was about to. I'd announce before breakfast, "I'm going to do my New Anthem!" because I wanted to make sure they didn't come into the bathroom while I was in mid-encouragement. I was afraid of getting caught in the act. What was I worried about? That my kids would see me believing in myself? What a terrible thing for my youngest daughter to find out about her dad. "Why am I in therapy?" she'd say to a friend years from now. "Because my dad had such a positive sense of self-confidence and hope. It was terrible."

When Ariel Gilbertson, a blogger from St. Francis, Kansas, felt uncomfortable repeating the New Anthem, she came to a very clear conclusion. "Honestly, if I can't do two minutes of facing the discomfort of saying nice things to and about myself (doesn't this sound silly out loud?), then I'm really not going to do the tougher things." The first step to being kind to yourself is always talking kindly to yourself. Self-care starts with self-talk.

Self-care starts with self-talk.

The good news is there's treasure hidden on the other side of discomfort. "In just two minutes," Ariel said, "we do something different which, done long enough, sets up a habit. One of these habits this little anthem accomplishes is changing the self-talk. The change in self-talk carries over to every second of our lives."

As you continue through the month, you'll realize that certain soundtracks stick out for you more than others. For Brad Wasserman, a wealth manager in Farmington Hills, Michigan, number 3 is what made the most sense. "I read it slowly and carefully that 'the only person standing in my way is me, and I quit doing that yesterday.'" That's the soundtrack that reminded him, "I need to stop standing in my own way and schedule my time to include priorities for my health and well-being so I can be effective for my family, my clients, my firm, and others." Even better than just retiring his broken soundtrack yesterday, he told himself, "I quit doing that [standing in my own way] on 8/31." He got specific with a date to reinforce the strength of the New Anthem.

Aimee Padgett, a wellness instructor from Moline, Illinois, loved the New Anthem but struggled with saying "I know I am my biggest fan." She found a creative way to fix her apprehension. She told me, "Okay, this is going to be a bit silly, but oh well! Football started back up, and as I am a diehard Chicago Bears fan, I started picturing myself acting toward myself as how I act about that team. I've had plenty of chances to give up on them (everyone who follows the NFL knows this), but I don't. And I won't. They're my team. I'm a fan. I cheer loudly about every game. I keep on hoping for the best. I create 'events' around their games (have people over, etc.) and invite other fans to join the fun. Well, now every time I say, 'I am my biggest fan,' I am reminded that the way I act toward myself is immensely important and attracts a certain type of atmosphere. I get to create my atmosphere."

Aimee essentially asked herself a powerful question: *What would happen if I cheered for myself as loudly as I cheered for my favorite team?*

Why Do You Repeat It in the Morning and at Night?

The reason you do it at least twice a day is that there are two slingshot moments you have access to: first thing when you wake up and last thing before you fall asleep. One launches you into your day and the other launches you into your dreams. For some people, the morning New Anthem had the greatest impact.

Dana Williams, a podcaster from Sugar Land, Texas, was most encouraged by this reminder every morning: "I've packed honesty, generosity, laughter, and bravery for the road ahead." She said, "These are areas I'm actively working on. I always picture putting them in my imaginary bag and love the thought that they're already with me. I just have to pull them out and use them." We're all deliberate about what we pack for trips, so why wouldn't we be with what we pack for our day?

We don't know how the day is going to go, but we know the volume of broken soundtracks is going to get raised at least a few times. You'll get stuck in traffic. A coworker will cancel an important meeting. A bill you weren't expecting will land in your mailbox. The dial will go up. In those moments, we'll use our turn-down techniques from chapter 3, but the whole process will be a lot easier if you set the dial where you want it to be before even leaving the house.

The morning New Anthem matters. So does the evening.

That's the one that Jeff Stein, a data analytics consultant in Spring Hill, Tennessee, got the most out of. "I feel like when I say my evening Anthem, it is so refreshing to know that I have 'left myself things to do tomorrow' instead of failing to get it all done."

Have you ever collapsed into bed with a long, incomplete to-do list? You feel like a failure in those moments because you mentally review all the things you didn't get done. What if instead you could listen to a new soundtrack and tell yourself, "What a day! The best part is that I left myself a lot of fun things to work on tomorrow."

We sometimes forget how important the last thing we do before bed is. Remember that weird dream you had after you watched a show about a mass murderer on Netflix as you were falling asleep? Remember another night when you woke up at 2 a.m. and scribbled down the solution to a problem because you went to bed thinking about it? Remember that time you couldn't fall asleep because you had a last-minute argument with your spouse right before bed? You're nodding along right now because everyone has had experiences like that. The final thing you do every day has an impact.

I think about my bedtime brain like a rock tumbler. Each night I have the chance to throw a few ideas in before I turn off the light. They'll bounce around for seven hours and sometimes—not all the time, but sometimes—I'll wake up with an even better idea in the morning. At the bare minimum, I will have done everything I can to set the dial where I want it before I fall asleep.

Waking up and going to sleep are **SLINGSHOT** moments. One launches your **DAY** and the other launches your dreams.

JON ACUFF

Want to Give It a Go?

If you want to get in shape, you have to exercise and change your diet.

If you want to write a book, you have to put your butt in a chair and plug away at the words.

If you want to build your business, you have to send proposals to clients.

Every new thing you want is on the other side of new actions. If you want to retire your broken soundtracks and replace them with new ones you love, you have to repeat them. Today's your chance. You've got a copy of the New Anthem. You don't need to wait until January 1 or the first of next month. You can start on a Tuesday in the middle of the year if that's what you want.

The instructions are easy. Read the New Anthem out loud to yourself in front of a mirror every morning and every night for thirty days in a row. Scratch off your progress on the checklist on page 217. Crossing things off on a list is the most fun you can have with a pencil unless you're John Wick.

When you try it a few times, you'll discover something surprising: you'll start to notice positive soundtracks in your day. Bright spots you used to miss will be a little more obvious, a little clearer, and a little easier to find. Catch as many as you can, because you're going to need them. A little bit of evidence is our best defense against one of overthinking's greatest weapons: the pocket jury.

9. Gather Evidence

The best part about the internet is that you can hire your heroes.

Everyone you admire is only one tweet or Instagram post away. In many cases, with platforms like Patreon and services like online coaching, you can even pay for a little bit of advice from someone who is farther down the road than you. That's what I did with James Victore in 2019.

Victore is an Emmy Award–winning art director best known for creating provocative posters and advertising campaigns. His work has been exhibited in the Museum of Modern Art, the Library of Congress, and a little building in France called the Louvre. He's also been a long-distance mentor of mine for years. By "long-distance" I mean he didn't know I existed, but that didn't stop me from learning from him.

In 2012, I bought his book *Victore or, Who Died and Made You Boss?* I read it several times, but what struck me most was a quote from runner Steve Prefontaine that Victore plastered across the back cover in massive block letters. It said, "Somebody may beat me, but they are going to have to bleed to do it."

That line became a soundtrack I used when I was building my blog. Whenever I felt like giving up or skipping a day, I'd repeat that line. I'd jump back on my laptop and think, "You might get more readers than me, but you'll have to write two million words because I'm going to write a million."

Seven years later, as I continued to work on my soundtracks, I was surprised to see that Victore was offering coaching. I'd been following him on Instagram @JamesVictore, and his entire account was a tour de force of positive soundtracks. Each post was a more enthusiastic declaration than the last. I leapt at the chance to do a video call with him but wasn't exactly sure what would happen.

People say you should never meet your heroes because they won't live up to your expectations. That's probably why I didn't ask Allen Iverson for his autograph in the Minneapolis airport. I considered it. I followed him through three terminals, trying to get my courage up, but ultimately chickened out. I think he would have been gracious, considering he was wearing a Sixers hat that said "Iverson" on the back. That's the absolute opposite of incognito. My plan was to open with, "Practice, we talkin' about practice?" and then ask him to take a photo where I lie on the ground and he steps over me like he did to Tyronn Lue in the NBA Finals. Come to think of it, it's probably better I didn't stop him.

I was a little nervous to talk with Victore, but my desire for help with my overthinking was larger than my apprehension, so I signed up for a session with him. I filled out a form on his website, answered a series of questions about my life, and then waited for the meeting date to arrive.

When it did, I had a long list of ideas I wanted to talk to him about. As soon as the video call started, I jumped right in and turned on a firehose of words. He kept trying to interrupt me, but that just made me pick up speed. Finally, I took a breath and he held up his hands. "Whoa. That's a lot. You're really bound up with fear."

That stopped me in my tracks. Fear wasn't the word I would have used to describe the questions I brought to our meeting. I wanted to argue with his assessment, but I'm doing this new thing where if I ask someone for advice, I listen to what they have to say. One by one, line by line, Victore started to break apart my list of ideas. By the end of the call, I realized he was right. The notes I brought to our conversation weren't dreams, plans, or actions—they were broken soundtracks. They weren't true, helpful, or kind to me, and Victore saw right through them.

For instance, I told him I couldn't be a good entrepreneur because my dad was a pastor and I never learned how to run a business when I was a kid. That broken soundtrack was telling me that because I didn't get business lessons in the first eighteen years of my life, like a father teaching his boy how to gut a trout, nothing I learned over the next fifty years could change that.

I read once that if you haven't learned a foreign language by the time you're ten years old, the difficulty skyrockets. Maybe I thought the same thing about owning a small business. *Dang, I wish my dad would've let me have that lemonade stand and do my own taxes in elementary school!* You can see how ridiculous that is when you read it, but I'd heard that broken soundtrack so many times that I believed it in my bones.

I took a lot of notes during our conversation, and then Victore got quiet for a moment. "I have a dare for you," he said, in the way that only an artist who looks like a pirate-poet can. "I want you to start saying a mantra that I've used for years." Once again, I'd bumped into a successful person using positive soundtracks to build the life they want.

"Say to yourself, 'Everything is always working out for me.'"

I flinched at first when he said that. It felt a little syrupy. It felt kind of fake. But Victore isn't that kind of guy. He's more punk rock than new age, more fight the establishment than skip through a field of flowers. He's a motocross-riding, New York City–dominating, take-no-prisoners kind of guy. I'd followed his career for years and knew he wasn't just giving me an empty platitude to put a pretty bow on our discussion. He was sharing a personal soundtrack he used in his own life that he felt might be helpful in mine too.

And he didn't want me to just say it once. He wanted me to repeat it. He wanted me to say it a dozen times, a hundred times, a thousand times if that's what it took to believe it. More than just saying it, he wanted me to look for it. To find examples of it. To point it out to myself and other people.

He wanted me to gather evidence.

You Find the Things You're Looking For

The reason "Everything is always working out for me" felt fake at first was that I didn't have any evidence it was true. I didn't have any proof. Worse than that, my pocket jury was telling me the exact opposite.

A pocket jury is a collection of broken soundtracks that judge your life whenever you dare to be more than you currently are. It can be built from criticisms by strangers, comments from friends, missteps, and missed opportunities. It often has reams and reams of evidence that you're not the right one to do that thing you're thinking about doing, but yet it's small enough to travel around in your pocket.

In addition to getting real loud whenever you try to work on yourself, the pocket jury also specializes in "record-scratch moments." Those are the intrusive thoughts that appear out of nowhere to remind you of some mistake you made four years ago.

That's what's so annoying about the pocket jury—there's no statute of limitations. It will pull out evidence

> **A pocket jury is a collection of broken soundtracks that judge your life whenever you dare to be more than you currently are.**

from ten years deep if that's what will knock you off track the fastest. That's why new soundtracks often don't last very long. We take this brand-new, bright-eyed soundtrack and send it into battle against a jury that's been preparing for this fight for years. Then we hope that the new soundtrack will somehow be louder than all the old ones.

Hope is a wonderful thing, but it's not enough if you want to really believe a new soundtrack. You have to gather some evidence of what you want to be true in your life. This is not

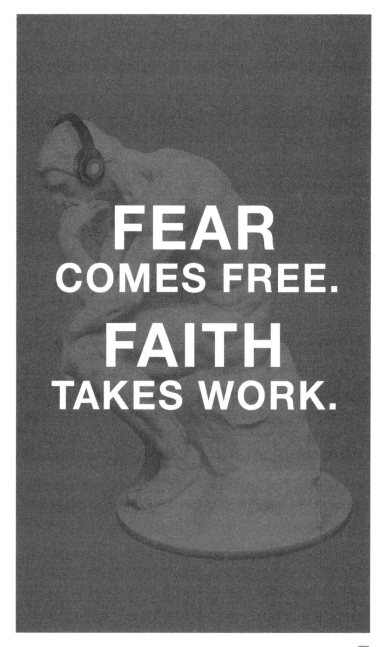

FEAR
COMES FREE.

FAITH
TAKES WORK.

a passive experience. Proof won't find you; you have to find it. Fear comes free. Faith takes work.

When you make a mistake, your pocket jury will automatically add that to the pile of mistakes you've made dating back to that time you got accused of plagiarizing from *Reader's Digest* in the seventh grade—a moment you still think about every time you write a book. That's a random example and not at all something that haunts me to this day, Mrs. Russo.

Gathering evidence, like every other action in this book, is not complicated. The easiest way to do it is to start with something every major city encourages you to do: if you see something, say something.

That was Victore's real dare for me. If I saw something that worked out, I needed to recognize it and then say, "Everything is always working out for me." Not once, not twice, but as many times as it took until that new soundtrack played as automatically as my old ones.

If a hotel let me check in to my room early instead of making me wait in the lobby for hours, I said, "Everything is always working out for me," and then I wrote that experience down in my notebook.

When a meeting got canceled, allowing me extra time to work on a project I was stressed about, I said, "Everything is always working out for me," and captured that in my notebook.

When a friend invited us to stay at his apartment in New York at Christmas instead of paying for an expensive hotel, guess what I said?

Everything is always working out for me.

The more I said it and the more I wrote down why it was true, the easier it became to see examples of it.

One morning we were headed to watch a family friend in a cheerleader competition. On the way there, they texted us and said the performance time had been moved from 9:30 a.m. to 10:50 a.m. Normally, I would receive that news like someone was purposefully trying to ruin my Saturday. Please refer to the previous seventeen examples I've given you of my soundtrack "People are trying to take advantage of me." What did the judges of an eight-year-old's cheer competition stand to gain by purposefully making my life difficult? Hard to say, but my broken soundtrack was pretty sure something nefarious was afoot.

This time though, I didn't listen to that. There was a new soundtrack in town that told me, "Everything's always working out for me." I didn't know how that was going to become true, but I decided to believe it was. I wouldn't end up waiting for very long.

Five minutes later, we found a beautiful coffee shop near the arena. Ten minutes later, we were all having avocado toast like we were millennials as we killed time before the event. The delay wasn't a bad thing; it was just an unexpected invitation to brunch with my wife and kids. Why? Because everything is always working out for me.

This wasn't just fake positivity either. Aiming for 100 percent positivity isn't even what's best for you. As Barbara L. Frederickson, PhD, says, "To experience 100-percent positivity defies and denies the humanness of life. It would mean that you'd buried your head in the sand."[1]

In her extensive research studies into the topic of positivity, Frederickson discovered a more reasonable goal. "Aim for a positivity ratio of at least 3 to 1. This means that for every heart-wrenching negative emotional experience you endure, you experience at least three heartfelt positive emotional experiences that uplift you."[2]

I was fascinated by Frederickson's scientific approach to such a traditionally squishy concept like positivity. It's one thing to say, "Turn a frown upside down." It's another thing to say, "Actively court three positive moments for every one negative." But that's exactly what Frederickson suggests in her book *Positivity: Discover the Upward Spiral That Will Change Your Life*. She writes, "This [3 to 1] is the ratio I've found to be the tipping point, predicting whether people languish or flourish."[3]

I knew I didn't need to look for the one negative experience. The pocket jury had that taken care of. Those were going to find me on their own. The three positive ones? That's a different story. Those were on me.

If you can't find evidence of your new soundtrack in your life yet, look for it in the world around you. For example, I screenshot typos that big companies make online. I'm not a grammar Nazi. Their so uptight, and its' easier then ever too freak them out if your interested. I collect typos because that's evidence to remind myself that "Momentum is always messy." If a company with ten copywriters, five editors, three designers, and two lawyers made a mistake in something they posted, maybe it's okay that I do too. Maybe instead of beating myself up next time, I can look at a few typos from billion-dollar brands, remember that momentum is messy, and be a little kinder.

The Three Steps to Catching Your Pocket Jury by Surprise

My teenagers are tired of how often I say, "Everything is always working out for me." If I get a particularly great parking spot at my youngest daughter's lacrosse game, I'll ask them, "You know why that happened?"

"Everything is always working out for you?" they moan from the back seat.

"Exactly!" I say, like I just won the parking lot lottery. After months of gathering my own evidence and waging war with my pocket jury, I wanted to see if that approach would work for other people. It had definitely reached foyer-idea status for me, and I was ready to test it out. I added the pocket jury concept to a thirty-day goal-setting challenge I was leading online and taught a few thousand people how to apply it.

The steps were easy. To beat a pocket jury:

1. Listen to what it's saying.
2. Gather evidence about what's really happening.
3. Tell yourself the truth.

Most of us have never taken the time to say, "Hold up, what is my pocket jury saying right now?" When we do, we're often surprised at the broken soundtracks that are playing. When Erin Corbett, a homeschooling mom from Akron, Ohio, did this exercise, she came up with a list of three things her pocket jury was shouting:

1. I'm not good at classroom-style learning.
2. I have very few marketable skills.
3. My lack of focus and organization habits keep me from successfully profiting from the skills I do possess.

She quickly recognized that her pocket jury wasn't being true, helpful, or kind. "It's super mean because I know I'm smart, but the pocket jury tells me it doesn't matter since I struggle putting knowledge to use."

Erin had completed the first step: she'd written down what the pocket jury was telling her. Now all she needed was an opportunity to gather evidence and tell herself the truth. It arrived in the most unlikely fashion, disguised as a broken refrigerator.

Her fridge decided to quit one day, as appliances are wont to do. Our microwave and dishwasher once stopped working in the same exact week. I'd like to think they went on holiday together, somewhere nice up the coast, but they probably don't even know each other since they're both pressed into the same wall and can't make eye contact. I called a repairman for both situations because I'm best at

To beat a pocket jury:

1. **Listen to what it's saying.**
2. **Gather evidence about what's really happening.**
3. **Tell yourself the truth.**

writing sentences about appliances, not fixing appliances. Erin decided to roll up her own sleeves instead and see if she could get her fridge to work again.

She did a quick Google search and diagnosed the problem. She bought a $38 replacement part from a store she'd never been in before and spent three days replacing the start relay. (I was going to recommend she look at the start relay as the issue or, like, the metal part that does the water thing—I knew one of the two was probably the culprit.)

That should have been a victory even the pocket jury could celebrate. She fixed the fridge. She saved the day. Hooray for Erin! Instead of admitting that she did an amazing job though, her pocket jury once again told her that she'd spent three days gathering more useless knowledge. It was another wasted skill and further proof that the things she knows how to do don't have any value.

Erin wasn't having it this time. She took the second step to beat a pocket jury and collected some of her own evidence to support her new soundtracks. Then she did step 3 and wrote down what was true so that it would stick:

1. I probably will never have to replace a start relay on a refrigerator again, but it matters that I did it once.

2. It saved me anywhere from $200 to $1,200 and that's worth it to me.

3. It's worth knowing the best parts guy in town and also knowing that if I pay in cash, it's cheaper.

4. It's worth fussing with a sharp screwdriver in a tiny space to disconnect the offending part from its locking

mechanism, because whoever made this fridge didn't want anyone fixing it themselves.

5. It's worth knowing that I can afford to put new groceries in the now-cold-again fridge, when just a few years ago this whole ordeal would have me finagling dinner invites from my mother and mother-in-law.

You can just see Erin throwing down each of those points in a courtroom as her pocket jury reels from the blows of this new evidence: *It matters because I say it matters. It saved me real money. I've got a parts guy!* If someone ever asks, "Do you have a good refrigerator hook up?" Erin can nod confidently and say, "I've got a guy." *I beat the manufacturer who designed it thinking I wouldn't be tough enough. I've made financial progress with my life and don't have to rely on free meals from my mother-in-law.* That's the strongest flex of the bunch.

I don't know if Erin shouted those five points at the fridge and then slammed the door like dropping a mic, but she should have. The money she saved in her battle with the fridge is great, but that's not the real value Erin sees from this exercise in overthinking. "The lessons I can learn from identifying pocket juries will be priceless if I pay attention to them and put them to use," she says.

It's time to put your pocket jury on notice too. It had a good run. It got to gather negative evidence for years. Cognitive bias has collected examples that reinforce your broken soundtracks without any resistance, but those days are over.

We've got the element of surprise on our side too. Pocket juries are always so cocky. They expect you to show up late to court, unprepared and disheveled. They've won for so long, they never see the loss coming—especially when you roll in with a secret weapon: effort.

Effort Is the Best Form of Evidence

What do you think is the second-best album of all time?

The best album of all time is undeniably Yanni's *Live at the Acropolis*, but I think there are a lot of good arguments to be made about that silver medal category. If you've never heard that album, I'm sad for your ears and your heart. Capturing it in words is like trying to spell the sound a hummingbird's wings make or describe a unicorn's breath using only colors, but I'll do my best.

Recorded in 1993 at the Herodes Atticus Theatre in Athens, Greece, the concert took eighteen months to plan. This wasn't the Rolling Stones at Madison Square Garden. Yanni (I honestly don't know if he even has a last name) had to woo the archaeological committee, mayor, and ministers of culture and tourism long before he could gift us a single synthesizer note. You ever get in a fight with your homeowners association because you wanted to change the color of your mailbox? Try throwing a concert in a temple from the Bronze Age. Everyone told him it wouldn't work, but Yanni didn't listen to the naysayers.

He invested $2 million of his own money at a time when Yanni's reported net worth was $2,050,000. You do the math. The only thing bigger than Yanni's mustache is his appetite for risk. You think he lorded that personal investment over listeners? He didn't. He just gave us unforgettable soundscapes like "Keys to Imagination," "Until the Last Moment," and "Reflection of Passion."

One year, I only wrote to that album. Every time I turned on my laptop I fired up *Live at the Acropolis* and was "Swept Away" (the ninth song on his setlist). I also found a way to become friends with one of Yanni's backup singers. I turned that into a chance to sit briefly on Yanni's tour bus with my mortified wife. (Yanni wasn't there. You think the first time you pick up a basketball you get to hang out with LeBron?) I still have a Yanni concert T-shirt in my drawer, having easily been the youngest person at that concert by an average of twenty years.

My love for *Live at the Acropolis* is real and spectacular. There's a good chance you don't like that album. That's not a big deal. Musical taste is unique to each person. What lights me up won't do anything for you and vice versa. The same can also be said of new soundtracks.

I don't know which ones you'll create. You can use all ten from the New Anthem. You can remix them into your own or start with a blank piece of paper and build a custom playlist. The choice is yours. There are a million positive directions you could head. It would be impossible for me to predict all of your new soundtracks, but I do know two that you'll hear. The first is, "That Yanni story was a long way to travel to get to 'Watch out for this specific broken soundtrack.'" That's fair. I accept that. But what can I say? Talking about *Live at the Acropolis* is "One Man's Dream." (That's track 6, by the way. How have you still not listened to that album?)

As we get ready to conclude this book and launch out on new adventures, the other broken soundtrack you'll hear is the one that asks, "Who do you think you are?" This is a classic pocket jury statement designed to keep you playing small. *Who am I to lead this company? Who am I to write a book? Who am I to manage this sales team? Who am I to raise kids? Who am I to be anything other than what I've already been?*

Jimmy Akers, one of the people I tested the pocket jury concept with, heard that question when he decided to launch an online guitar course. The beauty of the internet is that if you want to teach someone how to do something, you can. The barrier to entry is lower than ever because the technology has made leaps and bounds. The playing field is level. The pocket jury hasn't changed at all though. It's still a mountain every creator must scale.

Jimmy, a pastor from Fort Myers, Florida, was ready for it this time. He'd been through the pocket jury exercise with me. So instead of listening again, he gathered evidence and told himself the truth:

1. I have invested twenty-two years into learning and playing the guitar.
2. I have almost fifteen years of guitar teaching experience.
3. I spent over a hundred hours of preparation on this course.

Did you catch what all three of those have in common? Effort.

Each bit of that evidence was born from effort.

Jimmy spent twenty-two years learning and playing the guitar. He didn't just think about the guitar; he picked one up for more than two decades. Then he spent fifteen years teaching other people. Finally, he invested over a hundred hours building the course. He didn't beat his overthinking with more thinking. He beat it with more action, because that's always the path to victory.

A soundtrack without action is just a fortune cookie. It might be catchy, it might even be clever, but until you put it into action it doesn't accomplish anything. Jimmy had a great soundtrack. He told it to me: "I know how much of an impact this course could have." That's encouraging and super positive. That was helpful to have, but that wasn't all he brought to his fight with his pocket jury. He brought evidence built from effort.

If you have a new soundtrack you've fallen in love with, fortify it with effort so that if the pocket jury gets loud someday, you'll have all the evidence you need.

> **A soundtrack without action is just a fortune cookie: catchy, clever, but ultimately empty.**

In 2008, when I first believed "I think I can be a public speaker," I didn't have any evidence. How could I? I was just getting started. But I knew I wanted that soundtrack to play for years, so I focused on effort. I'm glad I did, because it turns out that the fastest way to make a new soundtrack true is to turn it into action.

I spoke at free events. I used vacation days from my corporate job to travel to conferences on my own dime. I practiced my speeches relentlessly. I became a content machine, turning out a million words on my blog. (I told you that you were going to have to bleed if you wanted to beat me.)

That's still my approach, because I haven't arrived yet. I'm outworking my pocket jury every chance I get. Twelve action-packed years later, I stepped offstage after a seventy-five-minute keynote at a dental conference in Orlando. The event planner said, "We had Seinfeld here last year, and you were funnier than he was today." Put that on my tombstone.

Why did she say that? It's not because I'm funnier than Seinfeld, obviously. It's because I met a salesman in the Nashville airport who was going to the same event. I chose to sit next to him on the flight down to Florida thanks to Southwest's open seating policy. I grilled him for two solid hours about his company, its product, and its culture. And then I killed at the event with the best dental jokes you've ever heard. They would bomb in every other room in America, but in that room they crushed. You think Seinfeld had jokes about hand tools, burs, or the Cavitron 300? Of course not. He didn't have to. I did, because the best way to shut my pocket jury up is to show up with overwhelming action.

I'm the one wearing neon-green Nikes while I finish this.

I'm the one writing down a win and shouting, "Everything is always working out for me!"

I'm the one who's asking your sales guy so many questions that everyone around us on the plane thinks I have a weird obsession with teeth.

I'm the one who is going to retire my broken soundtracks, replace them with new ones, and then repeat those so often they become as automatic as the old ones.

And I'm also the one who is going to teach you one last way to do all three of those things with my very favorite tool of all.

10. Make a Soundtrack Stick with a Symbol

The government makes you eat your steak well-done in Canada.

They should tell you that at the border so you can make a game-time decision about whether you really want to enter the country. That was one of two rules I learned when I visited Vancouver, British Columbia.

The other was that it's illegal to use your phone at the very first red light you come to after leaving the airport. It's probably illegal at every red light, but that's the one where they busted me in the least exciting sting operation ever.

My family and I had been in the country for about an hour. I hadn't made a single "aboot" joke or any derogatory comments about moose. We were headed to Whistler for a few days of summer exploration, and everything was rolling along perfectly. At a red light, I pulled out my phone to check on some orphanages I support. Or I was going to tweet. It was one of the two. I can't remember.

A police officer walked off the sidewalk and knocked on my window. I started to thank him for giving America Michael J.

Fox and Alanis Morrissette, but that's not what he wanted to talk about. "You can't use your phone in the car," he said. "I'm giving you a $300 ticket." Oh Canada.

I deserved that ticket. At the time, I didn't casually use my phone while driving—I was a power user. Responding to text messages is amateur. I was writing blog posts, capturing book ideas, and posting on social media with absolutely no regard for all the warnings on highway signs. Suffice it to say, I was not going to arrive alive and the text could not wait. If anything, I was surprised it took an international police force so long to finally capture me.

Out of Canadian kindness, the officer said, "It's not your fault. The rental car company should have warned you about our new rule. When you return the car, tell them to pay your ticket." That seemed like a terrible idea, but he had a gun, so I nodded along in agreement. He wrote me the only ticket I've ever received in my life and sent me north to the most beautiful mountains I never saw.

I missed that entire trip. I was there physically. I rode in the Peak 2 Peak Gondola. I hiked with my family. I ate a well-done steak that tasted like my shoe. But none of it could break through the noise of my overthinking. The second the officer told me to make the rental car agency pay the fine, I started rehearsing how that conversation was going to go.

Avis Agent: How was the car?

    Me: It was perfect. Great fuel economy. Huge trunk. Smelled nicer than I anticipated. It could not have been better. It worked from A to Zed. Haha!

Avis Agent: I'm so glad to hear that!

Me: (slowly sliding the crumpled ticket I've made damp with so much overthinking sweat across the counter): There's just one last thing.

Avis Agent: What's this?

Me: It's a ticket. Officer Fred wanted you to have it. I got it for using my phone while driving, and in a lot of ways, we both felt like that was your fault. So if you could have Tom Avis or whoever runs your company pay it, that would be great.

Avis Agent: Everyone, stop helping other customers for a minute and come hear what this guy just asked! Tell them what you told me. This is hilarious. You are the dumbest American we've ever met, and your steaks are dangerously undercooked.

That's just one version of how overthinking told me things would go. Each one was less true, less helpful, and less kind than the rest. How could they not be? Remember, I don't even like to ask autobody shops to do their job. Of course I'd overthink a conversation where I had to tell a rental car company to pay my traffic ticket.

"Look at that waterfall!" my wife would marvel as we drove up the Sea-to-Sky Highway, one of the most beautiful roadways in North America. "Stop overthinking the ticket. You can deal with it on Monday. You're missing this whole weekend."

"I am not," I'd reply. "Do you think the person at Avis is going to get physical with me? Is this the French Canadian side of their country, because if it is, they might hit me with a white glove across the face. I think the French love that sort of thing."

Three days later, I brought the car back to Avis and walked into the rental office. What happened next is going to surprise you. The actual conversation ended up being a lot easier than my overthinking told me it would be. A very polite Avis employee referred me to their customer service hotline and sent me on my way. Whole thing took about ninety seconds. I lost a three-day weekend over a ninety-second conversation. Has that ever happened to you? You got so lost in overthinking that everything around you became temporarily invisible? I made a whole coastal mountain range disappear, get on my level.

When I returned home to the States (that's how you say "America" when you've traveled abroad to exotic locales like Canada), I was able to put the conversation behind me, but not my habit of texting and driving. That part of the ticket incident was still bothering me. I knew eventually I was going to get in a car crash. Though months later Officer Fred canceled my Canadian ticket, I knew I'd start getting tickets in Nashville too unless something changed. Worst of all, I was on the verge of teaching my oldest daughter how to drive. If I didn't stop using my phone in the car, I was going to be a huge hypocrite every time I told her not to.

I had tried to quit before, but it was a hard habit to break. I'd put my phone in the trunk. I'd thrown it out of reach in the back seat. I'd turned it off while driving. Nothing really worked. I'd make it a few days but eventually find my phone back in one hand and the steering wheel in the other.

So, I did what any rational person would do in this situation. I went to the bank and got $200 in coins.

I Stumbled Upon the Power of a Symbol

I broke myself of the habit of texting and driving with a simple tool, but I've never written about it before because it's a little weird. As I researched this book though, I realized I wasn't all that special. I had just accidentally found one more way to repeat a new soundtrack.

That's really all I was aiming for. In the same way that I said, "I can be a public speaker," I was now saying, "I can drive without using my phone." In chapter 2, you asked your broken soundtracks the question "Is it true?" so that you could retire them. Now you're going to switch up the question a little bit to find a new soundtrack: "What do I want to be true?" I wanted to be the kind of guy who doesn't drive with his phone. I wanted to be the kind of dad who can teach his daughter to drive without feeling like a hypocrite.

Just like when I started the public speaking adventure in 2008, I had very little evidence I could beat my phone habit. Every circumstance in my life said the opposite. But I didn't just hope the soundtrack would work—I tied it to action. I knew I'd need a reminder or my new soundtrack would never stick. I wanted it to be simple, portable, and small. After a bit of thinking, I landed on coins.

Years ago, I bought a 1922 Peace Silver Dollar from a jewelry store on a whim. I kept it on my desk and would flip it whenever I felt stuck on an idea. I liked the way it felt in my hand. It was heavy. It was tangible in a world where most of my work isn't. Tweets, emails, Zoom calls—none of those things have a real weight. I also like how it connected me to a different era. Seeing "1922" on it reminded me that there was more to life than just today's challenges. Is that a lot to get from a coin? Yeah, I'm an overthinker. I really feel like that should be clear to you by now.

I decided that every time I drove without using my phone, I would give myself a dollar coin as a small symbol of my vehicular success. I didn't have any dollar coins in the junk drawer at home, where coins congregate like an elephant graveyard, so I ordered two hundred from the bank. It took about a week for them to come in from wherever it is that banks keep old-timey money. Fort Knox, I assume? The O.K. Corral? No idea.

The teller at the bank didn't think I was very odd when I picked up the money—at least not in that first visit. He just nodded, as if to say, "Here are the doubloons you requested, you suburban pirate," and slid a small box across the counter. There in the parking lot, I grabbed a roll with twenty-five coins in it and put it in my cupholder. From that moment on, for the next two hundred trips, I thought about my phone and the coins. When I'd pull in the garage after going somewhere, if I hadn't used my phone, I'd drop a coin into a big Mason jar that sits on my desk.

"It's your own money," my wife said one day as I unrolled another coin earned for a successful trip without my phone.

"What do you mean?" I asked, so proud of the fresh dollar coin I held in my hand.

"You're not earning money. You took paper money to the bank. You turned it into metal money. Now you're unrolling it coin by coin so that you can then someday reroll it and bring it back to the bank to turn into paper money again," she said.

"It does sound a little crazy when you say it that way, but I don't care, because it works."

That's a good summary soundtrack for my life: "It sounds crazy, but I don't care, because it works." It was certainly true in this situation. I spent three months going through every coin until all two hundred were in the jar.

By the end of the experiment, I was no longer using my phone in the car. The coin made my new soundtrack stick, so I did what I always do when I've stumbled upon a new way to win. I got curious.

> A fast way to find a new soundtrack is to ask yourself, "What do I want to be true?"

Why did it work?

Why did a coin help?

Why did something so small make such a big difference?

It took me months to find the answer, but when I did, it was so obvious.

It wasn't a coin. It was a symbol. And the right symbol can work wonders for a soundtrack.

You're Already Surrounded by Soundtracks

It took me forty-four years to learn what the best brands in the world have known for decades: symbols are a powerful way to cause action.

Don't believe me? Okay, then why do you think people put Yeti stickers on their car to let you know their preferred method of keeping things cold? Did you ever see someone put an Igloo sticker on their car in the 1990s? No one did that, but Yeti found a way to transform their product into a symbol.

Owners who never talked about a cooler before are now eager to identify with the symbol of Yeti. Over burgers in the backyard, they will quickly tell you that their cooler can keep meat cold for ten days in a row.

Granted, if you're ever in a situation where you are critically dependent on your ability to retrieve meat from a cooler and eat it nine days later, you probably have a bigger issue. There's been an apocalypse but you haven't been able to get to higher ground because your Yeti cooler is so heavy you can't move it. If you have a few guns, you can hunker down in the garage and protect it from outlanders, because it's also the most expensive thing you've ever purchased. The problem is that other survivors are going to know you have that cooler because you put a sticker on your car. At the time, it seemed like a good idea. How else would strangers know you were serious about portable refrigeration? Now, unfortunately, that sticker is just a beacon to other scavengers in the dystopian wasteland.

Yeti uses a sticker to encourage you to advertise their product on your car. Lululemon uses a logo to encourage you to buy their yoga pants. Nike uses a swoosh to ensure you hear the words "Just do it" without even reading them. Every successful brand in the world is serious about symbols because they know they work.

Symbols, and the meaning we attach to them, are powerful tools for living out our new soundtracks. The coins weren't special. They're small, an ugly color, and nearly useless. Good luck finding a vending machine in America that takes a dollar coin. I've looked, trust me. But none of that mattered, because the coin meant something to me.

It meant I was making my soundtrack true. It meant I wasn't going to get another traffic ticket. It meant I was keeping my word to my wife. It meant I was being a good example for my kids. I grew to love hearing the sound those coins would make when they landed in the Mason jar. I liked looking at the progress as the jar filled up. I started volunteering to run more errands for my wife because then I could drive again and earn another coin.

> **Symbols, and the meaning we attach to them, are powerful tools for living out our new soundtracks.**

It became a fun little game, and it turned out I wasn't the only one playing it.

Turning the Finish Line into a Symbol

There's a reason "dissertation" shares so many letters with "desert." Both are lonely, boring places where dreams go to die. (Sorry, Arizona. You know I'm right. Turquoise jewelry can only do so much.) The first part of a doctoral program isn't as isolating. There are more people involved in the coursework for the degree. You have professors, classmates, and a support network that moves you along.

But once you're finished with that part of your degree, you head out into the wasteland of your dissertation. Those can drag on for years and years because you're the only one pulling yourself toward the finish line. How do you know it's done? How do you stay motivated? How do you make it a priority when the rest of life gets loud?

Those were the questions Priscilla Hammond was facing in 2014. Her coursework was completed, but now she found herself in the desert of the dissertation. She wanted it over. She wanted her doctorate but felt lonely and distracted in this new part of the project. One day she heard a talk about grit. It wasn't just a talk, it was an invitation for her to start listening to a soundtrack: "I have the grit to finish my dissertation."

That's a great soundtrack, but listening once wasn't going to work. When you put a single new soundtrack up against something as daunting as a dissertation, it doesn't stand a chance.

Fortunately for Priscilla, the speaker did something smart that day. He brought a piece of finish-line tape for each audience member. He encouraged everyone to write on it what they were persevering toward. Priscilla didn't have to think hard about hers: "I wrote *Dr. Hammond.*"

She wasn't a doctor yet. That was still something in the future, but having that piece of tape added to the power of the new soundtrack. Internally, Priscilla was telling herself, "I persevere. I have grit. I finish dissertations." Externally, she was reinforcing that with the piece of finish line. "See, it says it right there. *Dr. Hammond.* That's going to happen." She didn't put the piece of tape in a drawer, because it's harder to hear soundtracks when they are buried deep in a piece of furniture. "I stuck it up where I could see it at my desk," she told me. It was a daily reminder of her finish line, a message in a bottle sent from the future.

It didn't change the amount of work she had to do. Using positive symbols doesn't mean you have to run fewer miles when you train for a marathon; it just means you might actually run them. Two years later, Priscilla finished her degree. "In 2016, I was able to write that [Dr. Hammond] as a fact, not a dream," she told me. She's now an assistant professor in South Carolina.

The tape was a symbol, and it worked for Dr. Hammond. Her story was just the tip of the iceberg though. When I started asking people if they used symbols, the stories came in droves.

Rocks, Reviews, and Tattoos

Everywhere I turned, I found people using symbols to make soundtracks stick.

Monica Tidyman, a library director from Stromsburg, Nebraska, has a rock on her desk. "My sisters-in-law and I hiked Fish Creek Falls at Steamboat, and it was a little tougher than we thought. At the top I picked up a rock and took it down to remind myself to never quit, because the beauty at the top is worth it."

Monica could hope she remembered that. She could hope that in the millions of thoughts she'll have every year, that one stuck out. She could cross her fingers that "Never quit, because the beauty at the top is worth it" will be the loudest soundtrack on the days she needs it most. Or she could grab a rock from the top of a mountain and put it on her desk as a reminder.

Erik Peterson, an author from Rialto, California, could hope he remembers his goals for his career, weight, marriage, and parenting. That's a pretty long list, but maybe he could remember them. I sometimes open my phone and then forget why I did—like standing in front of a digital refrigerator you can't remember the purpose of opening—but maybe Erik has a mind like a steel trap.

Or he could order dog tags engraved with all those soundtracks and wear them under his shirt every day. Guess which approach he's had the most luck with?

LaChelle and Darren Hansen, a married couple from Linden, Utah, could try to be positive when they get rejection letters from literary agents. That's part of the process of becoming a writer. You get rejected by agents, publishers, and strangers at book signings who decide $11 is too much for your life's work. The Hansens could just have "better attitudes." Or they could slap colorful stickers on each rejection letter that say "Good work!" and "Fantastic!" Then they could store all those rejection letters in a binder to help them remember that "rejection isn't failure, and it's not the end of a dream." "Someday," LaChelle promised me, "I will keep that binder on a bookshelf right next to all my published books."

A rock is different from a binder, which is different from a dog tag. There are a thousand different ways to turn soundtracks into symbols, but the ones people have the most success with share three similarities.

How to Build Your Own Symbol

If you want your soundtrack to stick, your symbol must be:

1. Simple
2. Personal
3. Visible

At least once a year, I almost get into bullet journaling. Originally created by Ryder Carroll, a digital product designer in Brooklyn, bullet journaling is supposed to be an easy way to track and plan your life. With an ordinary notebook you can work on your to-do list, your calendar, your expenses, the cycles of the moon, migratory patterns of birds, and a list of all the dogs you pet each month, complete with 3D illustrations created using Japanese felt-tip pens that cost more than the first car you purchased. It doesn't even matter what kind of car it was, because I promise it was cheaper than pale-vermillion markers made from wild boar bristles found only in the lowlands of Mount Fuji.

What begins simply often mushrooms with complexity until I don't use the notebook at all. This is the trap many symbols succumb to as well: the creation of the symbol proves more extensive than the benefit. To prevent that from happening to you, keep your symbol simple. Monica Tidyman picked up a rock from the ground. That was her entire symbol process. If you told me you weren't creative enough to come up with your own symbol, I'd ask you if you lived near any rocks. The answer is probably yes. The planet is covered with them. Each layer of complexity you add to a symbol allows

If you want your
soundtrack to stick,
your symbol must be:

1. SIMPLE

2. PERSONAL

3. VISIBLE

one more opportunity to get stuck overthinking. Cut that off at the pass by aiming for simple.

The symbol has to be personal, because you're 100 percent of the people who will be using it. A symbol that works for your husband won't work the exact same way for you. It has to reflect *your* unique soundtracks, not someone else's. While reading through the above examples, I guarantee that at least once you thought, "That's weird, I would never do that." Of course not—those are someone else's symbols. I personally wouldn't do the rejection binder like LaChelle and Darren. Looking at tangible examples of rejection would be discouraging to me. Personally, I never feel motivated by reading my one-star reviews on Amazon. Some people do. Good for them. That's their symbol, not mine.

Julie DenOuden, an elementary school teacher from Los Angeles, California, keeps a bag of lima beans on her desk. When she was in college, she had a professor whose husband was willing to paint lima beans for her first graders. It was a tedious, time-consuming task, but he did it because he loved his wife. That symbol stuck with Julie, and she realized she didn't want to settle in her dating relationships. She wanted a husband who would 100 percent support her—a husband who would paint lima beans. Her dad bought her a bag, and every time she sees it, she remembers there are great guys out there. That's such a perfect picture of a personal symbol.

Lastly, the symbol needs to be visible, because out of sight, out of mind. If you can't easily see your symbol, then it's not a symbol, it's a souvenir. Like that funny shirt you got in Panama City Beach that says "Pineapple Willy's." It's somewhere in a closet, forgotten the minute you got home and shook off the sand from that vacation. You need to see your symbol, especially in places where you're prone to overthinking.

April Murphy, a music teacher in southeastern Michigan, uses photos of her family as a symbol. "I post a photo collage behind my computer at work so I can see my family supporting me. Overthinking for me only happens when I feel isolated." That's a surgical symbol right there. She's attacking a specific cause of overthinking (isolation) with a symbol that combats it (her family photos).

> If you can't easily see your symbol, then it's not a symbol, it's a souvenir.

Your symbol needs to be on your desk, your fridge, your wrist, or even your body. Countless people turn soundtracks into tattoos as a way to forever emblazon some new decision. Paula Richelle Garcia, a photographer from Murrieta, California, has the word "joy" tattooed on the inside of her wrist. She says, "[It] reminds me that I get to choose how I am going to respond to every situation in my life." It might only be three letters in ink, but she knows that "the more I have practiced stopping my negative thinking in its tracks and started finding something positive in the situation (which can be very hard in the beginning), the easier it has become."

April Thomas, who described herself to me as "an auntie in Bel Air"—shout-out Fresh Prince—is a lot more blunt with the assessment of her tattoo. "I have a Bob Ross 'Happy Tree' tattoo," she says. "It slaps me back to the positive when I find myself in the upside down."

Sometimes the tattoo is an image, sometimes it's a phrase, but the meaning is always the same: "This symbol matters to me so much that I want to be reminded of it for the rest of my life." Talk about visible.

Do you know why the Lance Armstrong LIVESTRONG bracelets were so successful? Do you know why tens of millions of people wore them? Because they were simple, personal, and visible. Anyone can put on a bracelet—it doesn't come with an instruction manual. "So you're saying the arm part goes into this hole here? Run that by me one more time, please." It also meant something important to the person wearing it. If you asked about the bracelet, people would say things like, "I wear this to support cancer research because my mom lost her life far too young." I never met anyone who said, "I just don't like cancer, the noun. I don't personally know anyone who has been impacted; I'm just against diseases in general. Have you seen my eczema necklace?"

It was also extremely visible. Nike could have made it light gray. They could have made it a color that faded into the background a lot easier. They didn't. They made it bright yellow on purpose. And so should you.

Just Pick One

Years ago, when Mike Peasley, PhD, and I did our initial survey to see if other people wrestle with overthinking, I was surprised how many people couldn't finish it. It only took a few minutes to complete, but I got dozens of emails that said, "I only made it to question 3. I kept overthinking my answers."

That's probably the clearest sign that you're an overthinker—you overthink the overthinking survey. I understand how that happens and recognize that it would be easy to overthink this moment too. You could spend hours, days, maybe even weeks kicking around what would be the perfect symbol for your new soundtrack. Or you could pick one from this handy list I put together for you and move on.

Symbols You Can Use Today

1. An acorn to remind you that big things always start small. You can find those for free outside. Follow the squirrels.

2. An item of clothing that tells you "It's go time!" You don't have to get a cape—unless you've got a cape guy and can get one that hangs just right. But maybe there's a scarf you always wear on days when extra bravery is required. For ten years, I've owned "speaking jeans" that I only wear when I'm onstage.

3. A compass to keep you headed toward true north. You can pick one up in the camping section at Walmart or go retro and grab one in an antique store. Bonus points if you can find a nautical sextant to encourage you to keep looking out over the horizon.

4. A microphone. I didn't understand that I'd been using one as a symbol for twelve years until I did this exercise. I travel with my own mic. Every time I take it out of the case at events, it

reinforces my belief that I'm a professional. It's an earpiece that's custom molded to me, and it also tells the sound guys that I know what I'm about. Find a piece of gear related to your career or profession that gives you that same feeling.

5. A favorite photo you put on your phone's lock screen or computer's wallpaper. It could certainly be a photo of family, like April Murphy has, or it could be an object or a place you find inspiring. The rapper Drake (not to be confused with the duck) had a picture of a dream house in California that he wanted to buy when he made it in the music industry. Before he was even signed to a record label, that dream house was the wallpaper on his computer for more than five years. After staring at it for half a decade, he was finally able to buy it in 2012.

6. A framed quote you love. It takes about fourteen seconds to find motivational statements on the internet. Just keep in mind while you search, if a sentence sounds like something a fourteen-year-old girl would shout on TikTok, a fifteenth-century Italian painter like Michelangelo probably didn't really say it.

7. A strand of Christmas lights hung around your desk to add a little bit of all-year cheer. I have some hanging up in my office right now, because I realized thirty days of bright lights once a year wasn't enough for me.

8. An encouraging note from a friend. I have a folder of them next to my desk that I look at from time to time.

9. The first dollar your new business made. Did you ever wonder why restaurants and bodegas do that? It's because the money is a symbol that will encourage them to keep going when things get tough.

10. A pen you enjoy writing with. It doesn't need to be expensive or carved from ivory. I buy boxes of uni-ball micro blue pens a few times a year. They're cheap, but when I hold one, I feel like it's easier to write good ideas.

11. A plant you can actually keep alive. Skip the fiddle-leaf fig tree. Those only grow on Instagram. Try an aloe plant instead. I've had the same one for nineteen years. We bought it when we got married, and it's a reminder for me to keep growing our relationship.

12. A toy from your childhood. Have I talked about LEGO sets enough? That's fair. I also have a Matchbox car, a GI Joe action figure, and a small Waldo of *Where's Waldo?* fame in my office. It's easier to remember that fun matters when you've got a few symbols around you.

13. A Zippo lighter. I don't smoke, but in college I got engraved Zippos with two of my friends when we graduated. We put a quote from G. Love & Special Sauce on them, which was probably the first and last time someone did that at the Things Remembered store at the mall.

14. A mug from a trip. Starbucks makes this symbol impossibly easy to collect. When I started my public speaking career, I bought one in every city I traveled to as a reminder that I was building momentum.

15. A concert ticket, movie stub, ski pass, plane ticket, or any small piece of paper that reminds you of the adventures you've already gone on and the ones to come.

16. A piece of jewelry. I'm not a shark-tooth necklace kind of guy, but I would like to be friends with one someday. I'd accept alligator-tooth guy as well, if you've got somebody in mind. A bracelet, a necklace, a ring, or earrings are an easy way to add a wearable reminder to your life.

17. The race bib from the first 5K you ran. I've got a drawer full of medals in my desk from each race I did to inspire me to do more.

18. A seashell. The ocean always helps me remember that my problems are small in comparison to the Atlantic. Looking at the shell is also infinitely easier than finding the saltwater coastline of my home state Tennessee.

19. A Grammy. I don't have one yet because the academy won't acknowledge my audiobooks (politics), but I do have other small plaques around my office for things I've done successfully.

20. A check made out to you in the distant future. Jim Carrey wrote himself a $10 million check for "acting services rendered" when he was a struggling comedian no one had heard of yet. He carried it with him for years in the hope that someday he'd be able to cash it. Ten years later, he got paid $10 million for the movie *Dumb and Dumber*, and suddenly that symbol didn't seem so silly.

I bet you can find a symbol on that list that works for you. Now that you know what you're looking for, I think you'll be surprised to discover you've already been using one. Either way, strengthen the power of it by making it even more visible. A great way to do that is to share it online. Post it on Instagram with #soundtracks and tag me @JonAcuff so that I can cheer you on!

If You Find Me, I'll Give You One of My Symbols

If you still can't think of a symbol, come find me someday. I'm the ridiculously tall guy at the airport. When you do, I'll give you the one that's meant the most to me.

I loved that the dollar coins helped me quit texting while driving, but I didn't really like the design of the coin. It wasn't sexy at all. It felt like a dumb bronze quarter, not a symbol I wanted to keep in my pocket. That's when I remembered something the teller at the bank asked me when I picked them up. He did a double take when I requested dollar coins and asked, "Did you mean half-dollar?" I was confused at his question and told him the dollar ones would be fine, but weeks later I realized he was right. I did mean half-dollar coins.

When's the last time you saw one of those? They're a lot bigger than you remember. They've got John F. Kennedy's bust on them, there's a special bicentennial design, and some of them actually contain real silver. When you hold one in your hand, it really feels like something. When you flip it, it really shines.

I called the bank back and ordered five hundred.

Was that too many? Probably.

When I picked them up, all the tellers gathered around to get a look at the weirdo who had come back for even more coins. What was he doing with them all? What did he know?

They brought the box of coins out from the vault, and I was surprised to find out there'd been a small mix-up. When I ordered five hundred, they thought I meant $500 instead of five hundred coins. The box they had for me contained one thousand half-dollars. If you thought five hundred coins was too many, you should have seen the twenty-four-pound miniature coffin of metal I walked out of Wells Fargo with that day. I weighed it when I got home. That's not an exaggeration. That's math.

I started carrying a half-dollar with me every day. I put them in my car. I put them on my desk. I gave them to friends. As I did, I discovered something.

A coin looks a lot like a dial. When my broken soundtracks get loud, it's easy to take a coin out of my pocket and turn the dial down, reminding myself I don't have to listen to that loud music anymore. It even looks like a tiny silver record in the right light. And if I ever need to come up with a new soundtrack, I can do what we learned in chapter 6 and flip over a broken one. It was a symbol. It was a dial. It was a record. It was exactly what I needed to stay connected to the new soundtracks, and it only cost fifty cents.

That's the best news of all. You don't need to order a thousand. The bank will give you one if you want. And if you lose it, guess what? You're out fifty cents. I'll even front you the first one. I'm generous like that. If you see me at a coffee shop, I'll give you one. Trust me, I have PLENTY.

I'll admit, a thousand coins was too many. I didn't need that many. I'm glad I spent so much time working on my soundtracks though, because twelve years after that first message from the event planner, I got another one, and responding to it would require everything I'd learned about overthinking.

Conclusion

I'm glad they didn't mention Dolly Parton in the text message or I might have peed my pants a little in the coffee shop. Even without telling me the headliner, the speaking request was incredible.

"Will you do some comedy at the Ryman for our charity event?"

If you've never been to Nashville or don't follow country music, you might be unfamiliar with the Ryman Auditorium. It's affectionately referred to as the Mother Church of Country Music. It's the former home of the Grand Ole Opry and one of the most iconic music venues in America. From Hank Williams to Johnny Cash, Houdini to Bob Hope, everyone has played the Ryman since it opened its doors in 1892. (It was originally a house of worship, the Union Gospel Tabernacle, before becoming known as the Carnegie Hall of the South.) It's on every musician's bucket list and had been on mine since we moved to Nashville in 2010.

I was excited by the offer but also a little intimidated. In the corporate speaking world, I'm known for my humor. That's my niche, but I'm by no means a pure comedian. When I speak at a company, the humor often catches audiences off guard because the guy before me was talking about the intricacies of adjustable-rate mortgages. It's easier to kill in that context. At the Ryman, I'd be onstage doing straight comedy for an audience that was expecting a comedian.

This event was a different animal altogether. Plus, I wanted to live up to the family name. Roy Acuff, who was a first cousin to my grandfather, helped found the Grand Ole Opry. He was known as the King of Country Music and is featured extensively in the PBS documentary series Ken Burns did about the genre. There's even a statue of Roy with Minnie Pearl in the lobby of the Ryman.

I was already feeling a lot of pressure, and then they told me Dolly Parton was the headliner. I was opening for Dolly Parton at the Ryman. She's an American icon. She has her own theme park called Dollywood, wrote the classic "I Will Always Love You," and gave away 130 million books to underprivileged kids through her Imagination Library program. This felt like a once-in-a-lifetime opportunity, and I didn't want to blow it.

On the night of the event, I paced back and forth in the hallway like a caged animal. The comedian doesn't get a green room, so I just hung out on the side of the stage for five straight hours waiting for my two ten-minute segments. Famous country musicians kept coming up to me and saying, "You're the comedian? Have fun!" They'd all played the Ryman a dozen times and seemed completely at ease. I was focused on not panic-sweating through my sport coat.

When I met Dolly—or I guess you could say when I became best friends with Dolly—she was incredibly kind. I told her I was kin to Roy Acuff, and she lit up. "Oh! He was the king!" I thanked her for the opportunity and then tried to not sweat on her in the photo.

As I stood next to the sound board, waiting for my cue, I felt a long way from that first speaking request email in 2008. It had only been twelve years, but so much had changed. I lived in Nashville now, not Atlanta. I had two teenage daughters instead of toddlers. I'd written six books instead of zero. But one thing had stayed the same.

I was still listening to that same soundtrack that started all those years ago: "I think I can be a public speaker." I was still actively turning down broken soundtracks as they piped up. I was still using symbols like coins and neon-green sneakers to lock in my new soundtracks. I was still wearing my speaking jeans.

Without really noticing, I'd been retiring, replacing, and repeating for twelve years.

Although I was certainly nervous, I wasn't stuck by overthinking anymore. It wasn't getting in the way of what I wanted like it used to. I could see 2,300 people sitting out there in the dark, waiting for me to step into the light, and I knew I was going to kill it. My dental jokes wouldn't work this time like they had in Orlando, but I had some fresh bits about Dolly Parton that were about to crush.

After the event, a friend asked me an interesting question:

"Did you ever think you'd be at the Ryman opening for Dolly Parton?"

Do you know what happens when you listen to new **soundtracks?** You give your dreams more **time, creativity, and productivity.**

#soundtracks

I laughed and shrugged it off, but the truth hit me on the car ride home later that night.

Did I think I'd be at the Ryman opening for Dolly Parton? I did. I thought that.

In fact, at the beginning, the thought was all I had. Every step of the way, the thought was what I came back to. *I think I can be a public speaker. I think I can be an author. I think I can start a business.*

I couldn't have specifically predicted Dolly Parton or the Ryman when I listened to my new soundtrack for the first time, but I did think I could do events like that.

I think you can, too, because you're an overthinker. You're sitting on the most untapped resource in the world. Overthinking steals time, creativity, and productivity by making you listen to broken soundtracks. Do you know what happens when you listen to new ones? You give your dreams more time, creativity, and productivity. Not just a little—buckets.

What are you going to do with yours?

I can't wait to find out.

It might take twelve years. It might take twelve months. It might take twelve days. I'm not sure, but I know at some point I'm going to run into you at an event, at the grocery store, or online. And you're going to tell me about your turn-down techniques, your symbols, and the broken soundtracks you no longer listen to. Then you're going to tell me about all the new soundtracks you've got running through your life these days.

Mine told me I could be a public speaker.

It started with "I think I can . . ."

Whether you want to build a hotel, go from receptionist to CEO, get in shape, or chase some dream I can't even imagine right now, when you tell me about it, my reaction is going to be the same.

I think you can, now that you know how to tap into the secret power of overthinking.

The New Anthem Challenge

Each day this month do three things: 1. Read the morning anthem. 2. Read the evening anthem. 3. Complete one action toward a goal you've selected. When you do, fill in the boxes below. Get ready for a month of momentum!

I, _____, will _____.

1 ☐ AM ☐ PM ☐ Action	**2** ☐ AM ☐ PM ☐ Action	**3** ☐ AM ☐ PM ☐ Action	**4** ☐ AM ☐ PM ☐ Action	**5** ☐ AM ☐ PM ☐ Action
6 ☐ AM ☐ PM ☐ Action	**7** ☐ AM ☐ PM ☐ Action	**8** ☐ AM ☐ PM ☐ Action	**9** ☐ AM ☐ PM ☐ Action	**10** ☐ AM ☐ PM ☐ Action
11 ☐ AM ☐ PM ☐ Action	**12** ☐ AM ☐ PM ☐ Action	**13** ☐ AM ☐ PM ☐ Action	**14** ☐ AM ☐ PM ☐ Action	**15** ☐ AM ☐ PM ☐ Action
16 ☐ AM ☐ PM ☐ Action	**17** ☐ AM ☐ PM ☐ Action	**18** ☐ AM ☐ PM ☐ Action	**19** ☐ AM ☐ PM ☐ Action	**20** ☐ AM ☐ PM ☐ Action
21 ☐ AM ☐ PM ☐ Action	**22** ☐ AM ☐ PM ☐ Action	**23** ☐ AM ☐ PM ☐ Action	**24** ☐ AM ☐ PM ☐ Action	**25** ☐ AM ☐ PM ☐ Action
26 ☐ AM ☐ PM ☐ Action	**27** ☐ AM ☐ PM ☐ Action	**28** ☐ AM ☐ PM ☐ Action	**29** ☐ AM ☐ PM ☐ Action	**30** ☐ AM ☐ PM ☐ Action

Acknowledgments

Great books take great teams, and this one would have never seen the light of day without the following amazing people.

Jenny, thank you for never allowing me to overthink this book. I tried—oh, did I try—but you were a consistent, creative partner every step of the way. L.E. and McRae, the best part of opening for Dolly Parton at the Ryman wasn't being onstage. It was when the night ended and I got to come find you in the crowd. I'm so glad I get to be your dad. I love you! Mom and Dad, every time we talk you tell me that you love me and that you're proud of me. Thanks for showing me what it looks like to love life. Jon and Laura Calbert, I wrote half of this book at your house! I couldn't ask for more welcoming, generous in-laws.

Ashley Holland, I can't believe we've already worked together for six years. Everyone who ever meets you knows immediately that you're the real brains behind Acuff Ideas, LLC. MC Tanksley, you worked tirelessly to find the best stories for this book. Bryan Allain, twelve years of friendship with you feels like twelve minutes.

Huge thank-you to the entire Baker team. I have absolutely loved working with you and can't wait for the next book we do together. Brian Vos, thank you for stretching me as a writer. You're all over this book, and I'm so glad I got to go through the editorial process with you. Mark Rice, thanks for showing me how to serve an audience, not just sell a book. Amy Nemecek, details make or break a book, and you made sure mine were perfect! Patti Brinks and the team at Faceout Studio, you created my favorite cover of any book I've ever written. And you did it in the first round of designs! Dwight Baker, Eileen Hanson, Brianna DeWitt, William Overbeeke, Nathan Henrion, and the entire Baker sales team—planning this book with you in Grand Rapids felt like the start of an adventure, and I look forward to the next one. Mike Salisbury and Curtis Yates, thanks for guiding my career for the last eight years. Your input, especially during the proposal process, was invaluable!

Mike Peasley, PhD, your research turned fun ideas into real data that offers real hope. Thanks for lending me your expertise. Justin Johnson, Rob Sentell, and Kevin Queen, our Saturday morning runs helped shape this book in ways I couldn't have anticipated. Ben Fleming, this book wouldn't have happened without long, soundtrack-analyzing walks around the neighborhood with you. James Victore, Tom Ziglar, Patsy Clairmont, and David Thomas, you each gave so generously to this project, and I look forward to returning the favor. Everyone from the SeptemberJanuary group, thanks for testing these ideas and sharing your stories. Your words are on dozens of these pages.

Last but not least, Yanni.

Notes

Chapter 1 I Think I Can Do This

1. Seth Stephens-Davidowitz, "The Songs That Bind," *New York Times*, February 10, 2018, https://www.nytimes.com/2018/02/10/opinion/sunday/favorite-songs.html.

2. David Goggins, *Can't Hurt Me: Master Your Mind and Defy the Odds* (n.p.: Lioncrest Publishing, 2019), 352.

3. Alexis Benveniste, "This Is How Much Money Mariah Carey's 'All I Want For Christmas Is You' Is Raking In," CNN Business, December 17, 2019, https://www.cnn.com/2019/12/17/media/mariah-carey-christmas-money-trnd/index.html.

4. John Tierney and Roy F. Baumeister, *The Power of Bad: How the Negativity Effect Rules Us and How We Can Rule It* (New York: Penguin Press, 2019), 7.

5. Malcolm Gladwell, "Free Brian Williams," *Revisionist History* (podcast), June 7, 2018, MP3 audio, 21:00, accessed March 31, 2020, https://podcasts.apple.com/us/podcast/revisionist-history/id1119389968?i=1000413184954.

6. Ulric Neisser and Nicole Harsch, "Phantom Flashbulbs: False Recollections of Hearing the News about *Challenger*," in Eugene Winograd and Ulric Neisser, eds., *Affect and Accuracy in Recall: Studies of "Flashbulb" Memories* (Cambridge University Press, 1992), 9–31; quoted in Gladwell, "Free Brian Williams."

7. Romeo Vitelli, "Remembering 9/11," *Psychology Today*, March 23, 2015, https://www.psychologytoday.com/us/blog/media-spotlight/201503/remembering-911.

8. Jia Jiang, *Rejection Proof: How I Beat Fear and Became Invincible through 100 Days of Rejection* (New York: Harmony Books, 2015), 65.

9. Caroline Leaf, *Switch On Your Brain: The Key to Peak Happiness, Thinking, and Health* (Grand Rapids: Baker Books, 2018), 24.

Chapter 2 The Choice Is Yours

1. Daniel Kahneman, *Thinking, Fast and Slow* (New York: Farrar, Straus and Giroux, 2015), 53.

2. Kahneman, *Thinking, Fast and Slow*, 53.

3. Kahneman, *Thinking, Fast and Slow*, 54.

4. Michael Gelb, *How to Think Like Leonardo Da Vinci: Seven Steps to Genius Every Day* (New York: Dell, 2000), 5.

5. Barbara L. Fredrickson, PhD, *Positivity: Discover the Upward Spiral That Will Change Your Life* (New York: Three Rivers Press, 2009), 161.

6. Jon Kabat-Zinn, *Wherever You Go, There You Are: Mindfulness Meditation in Everyday Life* (New York: Hachette, 2014), 4.

7. "Re:Work," Google, accessed March 31, 2020, https://rework.with google.com/print/guides/5721312655835136/.

8. Charles Duhigg, "What Google Learned from Its Quest to Build the Perfect Team," *New York Times*, February 25, 2016, https://www.nytimes .com/2016/02/28/magazine/what-google-learned-from-its-quest-to-build -the-perfect-team.html?smid=pl-share).

9. Amy Edmondson, "Psychological Safety and Learning Behavior in Work Teams," *Administrative Science Quarterly* 44, no. 2 (1999): 350–83, doi:10.2307/2666999.

10. Jon Kabat-Zinn, "Mindfulness-Based Interventions in Context: Past, Present, and Future," *Clinical Psychology: Science and Practice* 10, no. 2 (2003): 144–56, https://doi.org/10.1093/clipsy.bpg016.

11. Herbert Benson, *The Relaxation Response* (New York: William Morrow, 1976), 12–14.

Chapter 4 Borrow from the Best

1. *The Tonight Show with Jimmy Fallon*, "Dave Chappelle Describes His First Encounter with Kanye West," YouTube video, 6:30, June 14, 2014, https://www.youtube.com/watch?v=R4SYIfhzMmU.

2. Deena Kastor and Michelle Hamilton, *Let Your Mind Run: A Memoir of Thinking My Way to Victory* (New York: Three Rivers Press, 2019), back cover.

3. Cindy Kuzma, "7 Things We Learned about Marathon Record-Holder Deena Kastor," *aSweatLife*, October 15, 2019, https://asweatlife.com/2015 /08/7-things-we-learned-about-marathon-record-holder-deena-kastor/.

4. Crispin Porter Bogusky Employee Handbook, https://www.cpbgroup .com/cpb-handbook-2018-12-12.pdf, p. 8.

Chapter 6 Don't Fight It, Flip It

1. Gordon Mackenzie, *Orbiting the Giant Hairball: A Corporate Fool's Guide to Surviving with Grace* (New York: Viking, 1998), 151.

2. "Tom Hardy: Bane Quotes," *The Dark Knight Rises*, IMDB, accessed March 31, 2020, https://www.imdb.com/title/tt1345836/characters/nm0 362766.

Chapter 7 Zig Your Way to Positive Thinking

1. Brian Koppelman, "Seth Godin 1/1/19," *The Moment with Brian Koppelman* (podcast), January 1, 2019, 50:28, https://podcasts.apple.com/us /podcast/the-moment-with-brian-koppelman/id814550071?i=1000426 814291.

2. "What Seth Godin Said about *See You at the Top* by Zig Ziglar," *This Is Broken* (blog), accessed March 31, 2020, https://www.thisisbroken.co.uk /books/see-you-at-the-top.

3. Christopher F. Chabris and Daniel J. Simons, *The Invisible Gorilla: And Other Ways Our Intuitions Deceive Us* (New York: MJF Books, 2012), 35.

4. Chabris and Simons, *The Invisible Gorilla*, 35.

5. Tom Ziglar, personal conversation with the author, December 10, 2019.

Chapter 9 Gather Evidence

1. Barbara L. Fredrickson, PhD, *Positivity: Discover the Upward Spiral That Will Change Your Life* (New York: Three Rivers Press, 2009), 32.

2. Frederickson, *Positivity*, 32.

3. Frederickson, *Positivity*, 32.

Jon Acuff is the *New York Times* bestselling author of seven books, including *Start, Do Over,* and *Finish.* He's an *Inc. Magazine* Top 100 Leadership Speaker, and speaks all over the world to companies such as Microsoft, Nissan, Walmart, FedEx, and Comedy Central. He's spent the last twenty years helping brands, teams, and individuals build the kind of companies and lives they really want. Jon lives outside of Nashville, Tennessee, with his wife, Jenny, and two teenage daughters, L.E. and McRae.

STARTING IS FUN,
but the future belongs to finishers.

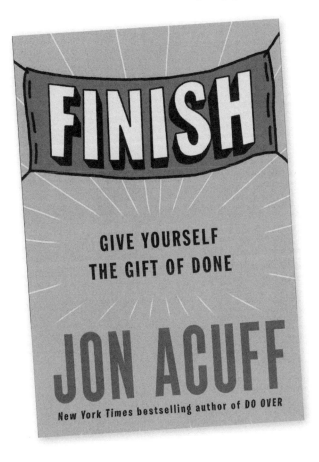

Tired of starting goals but never finishing them? You're not the only one. According to research, 92 percent of all New Year's resolutions fail. But what if there were simple, counterintuitive, fun ways to finish the things you start? There are. Find out what it takes to give yourself the gift of done!

BUILD THE DREAM JOB
you've always wanted!

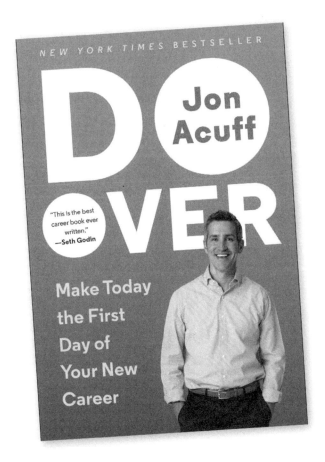

Dream jobs aren't a mystery. All you need to do is build a Career Savings Account™ with four simple investments: skills, character, relationships, and hustle. Let Jon Acuff show you what it takes to rescue Monday, reinvent your work, and never get stuck.

BIG LIVES START WITH BIG THOUGHTS.

Create Yours with the *Soundtracks* Course from Jon Acuff!

.

Building on the ideas in this book, Jon walks you through six compelling videos full of activities, exercises, and insights that will help you make the most of your time, creativity, and productivity.

Learn how to:

1. Get more done by turning up the music on every important project.

2. Make faster, smarter decisions with the flip of a coin.

3. Accomplish more goals by beating your pocket jury.

4. Improve relationships by picking the right soundtrack for the right person.

5. Create symbols and turn-down techniques that will make new soundtracks stick.

In addition to exclusive content, you'll get a beautiful workbook to guide you each step of the way.

Watch the free trailer at SoundtracksCourse.com!

5 IDEAS TO SHOUT ABOUT!

Every Friday I send out an action-packed, often hilarious collection of pure awesome! These are the kinds of ideas that if you came to my house for dinner, my wife, Jenny, would end up saying, "Jon, you're shouting about those ideas. Take it down a notch."

The ideas include the following:

1. Book recommendations

2. Songs you haven't heard but will undoubtedly love

3. Links to fresh videos

4. Things I think are funny

5. Tips on the little corners of life I know a little about (writing, speaking, entrepreneurship, parenting, Yanni, etc.)

And a whole lot more.

Don't miss a single issue. Sign up for free today!

Visit Acuff.me/newsletter

To see him live or to schedule Jon Acuff for your next event, visit BookJonAcuff.com

"It would be impossible for me to give Jon a higher level of endorsement. Over the past ten years Jon has presented to our groups on seven occasions and has been our highest-rated presenter each time. I have zero hesitation in giving you my highest level of assurances that Jon will have an incredible impact on your event."

—Ron Kitchens, Southwest Michigan First

"We would bring Jon Acuff back to Walmart anytime. He not only has executive presence, but he has lived the role and responsibilities. His ability to talk to any level is incredible. He is professional, honest, and human. He inspired our team and made the difference."

—Clara Park, Walmart International Support Team

"Akamai's marketing and sales leadership teams are still buzzing about Jon's talks. It's a testament to not only his obvious talent with humor and impactful storytelling in front of a crowd, but how he was willing to listen and adapt the content to what the teams needed to hear."

—Ari Weil, VP Product Marketing, Akamai

Jon is one of INC's Top 100 Leadership Speakers. He's spoken to hundreds of thousands of people at conferences, colleges, and companies around the world, including FedEx, Nissan, Microsoft, Lockheed Martin, Chick-fil-A, Nokia, and Comedy Central. Known for his insights wrapped in humor, Jon always provides a mix of inspiration and instruction that leaves audiences ready to turn their ideas into actions.

CONNECT WITH JON ONLINE!

LIKE THIS BOOK?

Consider sharing it with others!

- Share or mention the book on your social media platforms using **#soundtracks**.

- Write a book review on your blog or on a retailer site.

- Pick up a copy for friends, family, or anyone who you think would enjoy and be challenged by its message!

- Share this message on Twitter, Facebook, or Instagram:
  I loved **#soundtracks** by **@jonacuff** // **@ReadBakerBooks**

- Recommend this book for your church, workplace, book club, or class.

- Follow Baker Books on social media and tell us what you like.

f ReadBakerBooks

🐦 ReadBakerBooks

📷 ReadBakerBooks